KT-160-263

Routledge Introductions to Development

Series Editors:
John Bale and David Drakakis-Smith

Ecology and Development in the Third World

NEWMAN COLLEGE
BARTLEY GREEN
BIRMINGHAM, 32.

CLASS 333.7091724
ACCESSION 91458
AUTHOR GUP

In the same series

Term-time opening hours:

Thurs: 9.00 - 8.00 pm

WITHDRAWN

N 0015900 X

Avijit Gupta

Ecology and Development in the Third World

ROUTLEDGE

London and New York

To my father

First published in 1988 by
Routledge
11 New Fetter Lane, London EC4P 4EE

Published in the USA by
Routledge
in association with Routledge, Chapman and Hall, Inc.
29 West 35th Street, New York NY 10001

© 1988 Avijit Gupta

Printed in Great Britain by
Richard Clay Ltd, Bungay, Suffolk

All rights reserved. No part of this book may be reprinted or reproduced or utilized in any form or by any electronic, mechanical or other means, now known or hereafter invented, including photocopying and recording, or in any information storage or retrieval system, without permission in writing from the publishers.

British Library Cataloguing in Publication Data

Gupta, Avijit
Ecology and development in the Third World.
—(Routledge introductions to development).
1. Human ecology—Developing countries
2. Developing countries—Economic
conditions
I. Title
304.2'09172'4   HC59.7

ISBN 0–415–00673–2

Library of Congress Cataloging in Publication Data

Gupta, Avijit.
Ecology and development in the Third World / Avijit Gupta.
p.   cm. — (Routledge introductions to development)
Bibliography: p.
Includes index.
ISBN 0–415–00673–2 (pbk.)
    1. Environmental policy—Developing countries.   2. Developing
countries—Economic policy—Environmental aspects.   3. Natural
resources—Developing countries.   4. Environmental protection—
Developing countries.   I. Title.   II. Series.
HC59.72.E5G86 1988
363.7'056'091724—dc 19

Contents

Preface

The improvement in the living conditions of the inhabitants of the Third World involves both economic growth and the ambient ecological conditions. These two factors need not be in conflict, and development of a country implies improvement in both spheres. This slender volume is an attempt to introduce the reader to the problems that are created when the ecological side of development is neglected. Attention is also drawn to the fact that we all share the same planet, that the environment is a wonderfully integrated system, and that any large-scale ecological misdemeanour may result in an ecodisaster for all of us.

I found my education and work experience in both the First and Third Worlds extremely useful in writing this book. I am also fortunate in having been taught for a few years in a university department which happens to bring together the two disciplines of geography and environmental engineering, an extremely uncommon combination, but very helpful in preventing one from looking at the environment from the narrow viewpoint of one's own interest.

I should like to acknowledge my debts to several individuals without whose help and encouragement this book probably would not have been finished. I am obliged to Irene Chee and Peh Mung Ngian for typing the manuscript, and to Lee Li Kheng for drafting the diagrams with the usual speed and efficiency. The book has improved considerably from the criticisms on an earlier draft by A. Fraser Gupta, Mukul Asher, and Richard Corlett. I should also like to thank the organizations and individuals who gave me permission to reproduce their illustrations. Their names are included in the captions.

Lastly I should like to thank Anthea and Ella for their tolerance of my unsocial behaviour for the couple of months when the bulk of this book was written.

1
Introduction

The purpose of the book

The countries of the Third World, with a few exceptions, possess certain characteristics in common. Most of the countries are in the tropics. Economically they are at a less developed state than the countries of western Europe or North America or Japan. They usually carry a large population, if not in absolute terms, at least relative to the opportunity offered by the environment. In general, the economy is based on agriculture including herding, or on the extraction of timber or mineral products. Their progress is hampered by disadvantages, such as a lack of natural resources or technical expertise, inefficient transport networks, indebtedness to international financial organizations or developed nations, and a lack of power and influence in the international economic and political arrangements.

Within this general picture, however, there is a wide diversity. India, for example, has the second largest population in the world, over 750 million in an area of 3,288 thousand km², with a juxtaposition of intense population pressure, low per capita income, self-sufficiency in food production, an established industrial base, and technical expertise sufficient to generate nuclear power and launch space satellites. Tanzania, with an area of nearly 950,000 km² and over 21 million people, has an agricultural base, and in spite of the existing power and mineral resources, an underdeveloped industrial sector. Papua New Guinea, with a scattered population of about 3.5 million in a vast area of mountains, valleys, and coastal plains, is dependent on traditional agricultural practices and extraction of forest timber or minerals, such as gold and copper. At the other extreme, Singapore is a small prosperous city state of about 600 km^2 and about 2.5 million inhabitants, a very high per capita income, and well-established service industry, but very heavily dependent on foreign technology and import of agricultural produce.

The Third World countries are trying to improve the living conditions of their citizens. However, the steps taken to achieve this, the logging of timber, the extraction of mineral resources, the expansion and intensification of agriculture, the establishment of industries, may all occur simultaneously with a progressive deterioration of the environment.

The tropical ecosystem is a fragile environment and, especially in relation to the fertility of the soil, is easily disturbed. However, environmental degradation with development has happened throughout history. The ruining of the soils of Mesopotamia several thousand years ago by the establishment of an irrigation system which brought salt up from the saline groundwater to the agricultural fields is a good example. The amount of degradation has reached alarming proportions in the developed countries. There, over the last twenty-five years or so, the folly of development without an assessment of the environmental impact has been progressively realized, and laws enacted to prevent runaway ecological disasters from taking place. A century ago George Perkins Marsh said, 'Man has too long forgotten that the earth was given to him for usufruct alone, not for consumption, still less for profligate waste'. As the Third World countries attempt to improve their economic conditions, they are also contributing to the degradation of the environment in the world.

Improved economic conditions, however, are crucial to the Third World, where they are needed to improve the quality of life or, in some extreme cases, to prevent starvation. It is thus necessary to remove timber from the forests, extract minerals from the surface rock layers, expand farming into areas of unreliable rainfall or steep slopes, and establish industries of various types. It is also necessary to review such projects before and after implementation so that the deterioration of the environment, if it cannot actually be prevented, can at least be controlled. The purpose of this book is twofold. First, it provides an account of the nature of ecological degradation associated with development in the Third World; and second, it reviews the steps that could be taken to prevent or reduce such deprivation. The preventive steps are usually a collection of technical, social, and economic measures.

2
Development and natural vegetation

The natural vegetation

Three large regions of rainforest occur in the Amazon Basin, Equatorial Africa, and south and south-east Asia (figure 2.1). Away from the rainforest areas, where rainfall decreases and becomes seasonal, the rainforest is replaced by tropical monsoon forest, tropical grassland with trees, a poorer type of tropical grassland, and finally by semidesert scrubland. The vegetation outside the rainforest has been greatly destroyed, and survives only in protected or relatively inaccessible areas.

Traditionally the inhabitants of the rainforest have been hunters and gatherers or shifting cultivators. In the latter type of livelihood, patches of the forest are cleared by cutting and burning, and crops such as yam, cassava (also called tapioca and manioc), bananas, and sweet potato, are planted. In spite of the luxuriance of the forest the soils are usually infertile, and are kept productive only by the continuous decomposition of the fallen leaves and branches. Once cleared, the productive capacity of the land decreases in a few years, weeds start to establish themselves, and the cleared plots are abandoned for newer patches. The old clearings are soon under a secondary growth of vegetation, which starts to replenish the soil with nutrients, thus permitting a recultivation of the plots after a gap of years.

With development, however, rainforests are perceived as a storehouse of resources, mainly timber and charcoal or firewood. Between such extractive activities and cultivation of both shifting and sedentary types, the rainforests

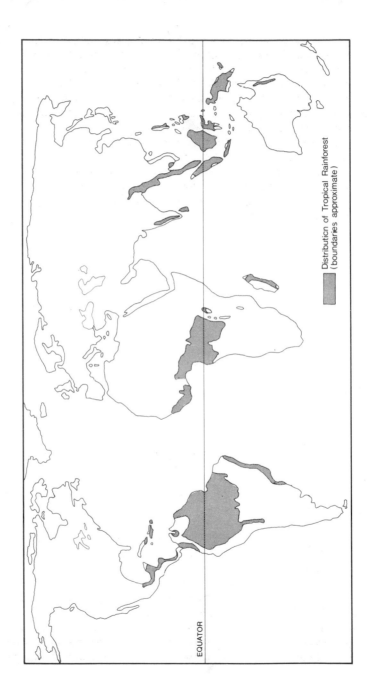

EQUATOR

Distribution of Tropical Rainforest
(boundaries approximate)

Figure 2.1 Distribution of the rainforests of the world

of the world are shrinking at a rapid rate. Each year thousands of square kilometres of deforestation occur in Central and South America (figure 2.2), south-east Asia, and Africa. It has been estimated by various researchers that by the year 2000 the rainforest will disappear from most of its present location. The situation for the other types of tropical vegetation is even grimmer: they are being rapidly destroyed in the search for new agricultural land and for fuelwood.

The forests of the developed countries on the other hand are stable with a total area of about 20 million km^2. The destruction of the forests happened earlier, and at present the remnants are preserved and managed as reasonably stable forest resource bases. The amount of timber extracted is monitored and is balanced by new planting elsewhere in the forest. Pressure for agricultural expansion is also nonexistent.

The demand for the resources of the forest

Apart from the denudation of the land due to timber extraction and agricultural expansion, tropical forests are also destroyed when mineral resources are discovered in the area, or new highways and settlements are built. The extraction of wood is carried out at two different levels of economy. Tropical hardwood is extracted as an industrial raw material, and fuelwood is gathered by the poorest sections of the community.

Extraction of timber

Since the 1950s the extraction and export of tropical hardwood to Europe, Japan, and the USA have increased tremendously. The light hardwoods of the south-east Asian forest have been harvested at an alarming rate, especially in Indonesia, Malaysia, and the Philippines. Huge timber concessions have been granted, for example the Madang timber project in the Gogol Basin in Papua New Guinea, where a Japanese company is extracting timber from a lowland rainforest for preparation of wood chips. Again, tropical hardwoods provide a relatively homogeneous surface, and because of the tree dimensions it is possible to produce large planks of uniformly high quality, which have numerous uses in the timber industry. The destruction of the forest is not restricted to the taking out of the valuable timber species. Collection of timber requires construction of roads, and when the large trees fall they destroy the vegetation in the vicinity. Almost all of the lowland forests of peninsular Malaysia will probably disappear in this century. The tropical bamboo forests are under similar threat, bamboo being the raw material for the paper industry. Figure 2.3 shows the distance from which bamboo is collected for an Indian paper mill.

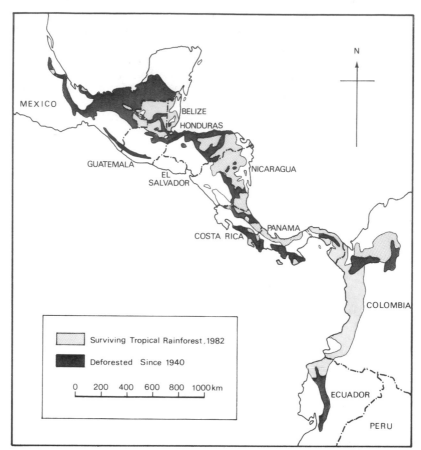

Lowland and lower montane tropical rainforests in Central America (Mid – 1983)

Country	Undegraded rainforest km²	Current rate of loss per year km²	Major threats
Nicaragua	27 000	1 000	cattle ranching
Guatemala	25 700	600	colonization, cattle ranching
Panama	21 500	500	cattle ranching, logging
Honduras	19 300	700	cattle ranching, colonization
Costa Rica	15 400	600	cattle ranching
Belize	9 750	32	colonization
Mexico	7 400	600	cattle ranching, colonization
El Salvador	0	0	(deforested)
TOTAL	126 050	4 032	

Figure 2.2   Destruction of rainforests in Central America [From J.D. Nations and D.I. Komer (1983) 'Central America's tropical rainforests: positive steps for survival', *Ambio* 12 (5), 232–8, cartographer: J.V. Cotter]

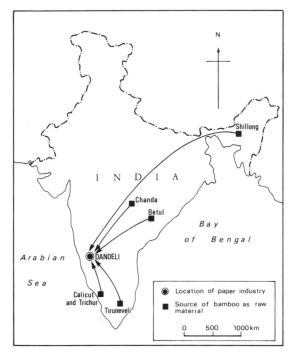

Figure 2.3 Distance over which bamboo is collected for a paper industry near the west coast of India [From A. Agarwal and S. Narain (eds) (1986) *The State of India's Environment 1984–5*, New Delhi, Centre for Science and Environment]

Collection of firewood

At the other end of the economic spectrum, forests, especially those in drier areas, are being reduced by the collection of fuelwood. Fuelwood and charcoal are the main sources of energy for the large number of poor of the Third World. The use of fuelwood is extremely important in Nepal, India, China, Kenya, Zimbabwe, Brazil, and Egypt, to name just a few examples. Every possible form of biomass is used: wood, twigs, crop residues, grass. If wood is difficult to procure, dried dung of domestic animals is used, thereby depriving the agricultural fields of animal manure. In the Himalayan Mountains, groups of women are forced to climb from the villages in the valleys to forests on the upper slopes to collect firewood. The time required disrupts family stability, and shortens the time for what in other areas would be considered a normal day's household chores. Similar collection goes on in the African Highlands or in the desert fringes of the Third World. As deforestation spreads, collecting firewood becomes more and more difficult

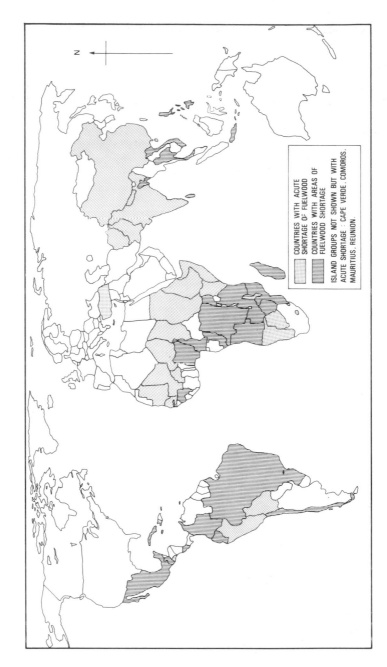

Figure 2.4 Depletion of fuelwood in the Third World [Classification of countries based on World Resources Institute listing]

The legend in the figure reads:

COUNTRIES WITH ACUTE SHORTAGE OF FUELWOOD

COUNTRIES WITH AREAS OF FUELWOOD SHORTAGE

ISLAND GROUPS NOT SHOWN BUT WITH ACUTE SHORTAGE : CAPE VERDE. COMOROS. MAURITIUS. REUNION.

over a very large part of the Third World (figure 2.4). Fuelwood is in demand even in the cities, where it is hauled from distant forests.

Agricultural practices

Deforestation is also caused by agricultural practices. The increase in the number of shifting cultivators necessitates a return to the old plots before the soil has had time to regenerate itself. Poor landless peasantry tends to move into the edges of the forest in search of farming areas. Since the seventeenth century large areas of tropical forests have been cleared for plantations in all the three continents concerned. For example rubber and oil palm have replaced the rainforest on the lower slopes of Malaysia. The latest addition to the list are the cattle ranchers in the American rainforest. In Central America beef cattle are raised on pastures derived from the rainforest, a practice which is also found in the Amazon Basin. The lean meat from the grassland cattle is used in the hamburgers, hot dogs, and canned meat industries of the USA. The demand for lean meat is met at a much lower cost than that incurred by raising the beef in the traditional US cattle country. Jackson has pointed out that in 1981 one-third of Costa Rican land was under ranching, primarily for export of beef to the USA. Similar cattle ranching expansion has occurred in parts of Africa in response to the demands of the European Economic Community.

Miscellaneous demands on the rainforest

The forest is also destroyed by other activities. Mining on a large scale such as for the iron ores of Carajas in Brazil or the Bailadila area of Bastar district, India, destroys the flora and fauna over a large area. New highways like the .Trans-Amazon Highway or the Trans-Sumatra Highway cut through virgin forest, and bring in settlers, often as part of a government enterprise (as in the Indonesian *transmigrasi* project). Deforestation is the final result of all such demands on the land and resources of the tropical rainforest.

The effects of the deforestation

There are two basic problems in the evaluation of the extent of the global ecodisaster of deforestation. First, the data supplied by the governments of various countries are usually a few years out of date and the area of deforestation is understated. A better estimation is perhaps possible with remote sensing. On the island of Borneo in 1982–3, the extent of damage from the catastrophic fire, which was apparently triggered by burning for land clearance during the dry season and which destroyed nearly 35,000 km^2 of forest, was measured from satellite photographs. The second evaluation problem relates to the multiscale effects of deforestation. The local impacts such as increased soil erosion, decrease in fertility, and loss of flora and fauna are better known than the long-term and global effects of large-scale deforestation.

Soil erosion and depletion

The immediate effect of clearing the forest is accelerated soil erosion which not only ravages the surface in a network of gullies, but also greatly increases the sediment load of the local streams, often choking them with bar formations. Less water infiltrates into the ground after forest clearance, especially if heavy equipment has been used, as such equipment compacts the surface. This increases runoff over the surface, and the eroded sediment and water is quickly and simultaneously transported to the sediment-choked river, causing it to overflow. An increase in flooding as a consequence of deforestation is to be expected. If steep slopes are cleared of forests, landslides start to occur in high frequency. Data from various parts of the world indicate that forest removal increases erosion easily by a hundred times or more by volume of material removed. As mentioned earlier, organic matter and other nutrients of the soil are quickly lost and not naturally replenished, leading to rapid declines in crop yields. Overgrazing in drier areas destroys the scattered vegetation leading to the same results of soil erosion and depletion.

Loss of local flora and fauna

Apart from timber, tropical forests supply oils, gums, rubber, fibres, dyes, tannin, resins, and turpentine. They are also sources of many varieties of fruits and ornamental plants. Many of the tropical rainforest species have not been properly examined, or even discovered. Some of the known ones are of tremendous importance. For example, tropical forests provide ingredients for drugs for leukaemia and Hodgkin's disease, and contraceptive pills. They also supply strychnine, ipecacuanha, reserpine, curare, quinine, and diosgenin – all invaluable raw materials for the pharmaceutical industries. Species from the tropical forest have been used in the hybridization of cereals which are responsible for the Green Revolution. This great gene pool of the tropical forests should be preserved. The forests are also home for a vast number of fauna, and the destruction of the rainforest is likely to result simultaneously in the elimination of a large number of such species.

The macro-scale consequences

The global and long-term effects are not clearly understood yet, but certain consequences are feared. The loss of the forest decreases the moisture in the soil, and is also expected to lead to a reduction in the rainfall of the region leading to changes in the flow patterns of local rivers. The surface of the deforested land reflects a greater amount of solar energy back to the atmosphere. A macro-scale deforestation like that of the Amazon Basin may lead to changes in atmospheric heat flux and rainfall pattern on a global scale.

The biggest modification of the earth's climate is expected to come from an increase in carbon dioxide in the atmosphere following widespread deforestation. Such an increase on a global scale may provide enough carbon dioxide in the atmosphere to absorb sufficient thermal infrared radiation to cause a worldwide rise in temperature, the so-called greenhouse effect. This might cause melting of the Antarctic and Greenland ice sheets and concomitant flooding of the low coastal areas of the world. There is considerable uncertainty regarding this prediction for various reasons, but it is a possibility that has to be considered. Even changes in global patterns of rainfall are possible, which may alter the distributions of the regions of agricultural prosperity.

Managing the ecodisaster

The management problem is the dilemma of preserving the forests of the Third World as an invaluable component of the physical environment or using them as resources for short-term economic improvement. Not only does the destruction of forests provide fuelwood and land, albeit temporarily, to the poor, but also the extraction of timber supplies the governments concerned with revenue, often as foreign exchange. Myers is of the opinion that the pressure of international debt has served to promote cattle ranching in the Amazon Basin, to reduce logging restrictions in Ecuador, the Ivory Coast, and Indonesia, and to expand the growing of cash-producing non-food crops on farmlands thereby driving the subsistence farmers into more fragile environments in the Sahel countries. There is thus a strong conflict between proper management and the desire for an immediate trading or subsistence resource which could be used for national development.

Several techniques are being practised for a better management of the resources of the tropical rainforests. Agroforestry where shade-tolerant crops are grown in conjunction with the forest trees is one example. Crops grown in various parts of the world in this fashion include cocoa, rubber, palms, cacao, cassava, maize, and green legumes. The cultivation is done in small plots which can integrate with the forest, and can support the poor peasantry living in or near the rainforest itself.

Cleared land not in agricultural use can be reforested with species suitable for contributing fuelwood which is in great demand (figure 2.4). The land remains vegetated, but there is enough opportunity to collect fuelwood for energy by people who would otherwise be compelled to go to undisturbed areas of vegetation in search of fuel. Such forestry practices which go beyond the standard techniques of forest preservation, and make a direct contribution to the well-being of the society are known as social forestry. An example of this is given in case study A.

Large-scale projects such as regional logging operations, construction of highways or transmigration of farmers in the rainforest are carried out under government supervision, and should be carefully monitored with a view to preventing destructive environmental impact of such projects on the fragile environment of the rainforest. Such projects are not always even economically successful, and in the long run may deprive the country of its natural resources. Imports of forest products are increasing in some developing countries. Until 1974 Nigeria was an exporter of forest products

Case study A

Social forestry in India

In India social forestry programmes have been started by several state governments in order to provide fuelwood, fodder, small timber, and minor forest produce to the rural people. Social forestry in India has three aspects: (1) farm forestry, where the farmers are supplied with free or subsidized seedlings in order to encourage them to plant more trees on their land, (2) community woodlots, where village communities are encouraged to plant trees on common lands to be equally shared, and (3) forestry woodlots, where trees are planted for the community by the government forestry department on public lands such as along the roads or banks of canals. In general, it looks like a successful project in many areas, but there are three areas where criticism has been levelled at the system. First, the programme, which is expected to use short rotation trees as a cash crop, tends to benefit prosperous farmers more than the poorer section of the community; second, the community woodlot part of the programme is not progressing successfully; and third, the extensive use of eucalyptus as a cash crop undoubtedly provides fuelwood but by lowering the water table it depletes the soil of nutrients and in general degrades the area ecologically. The advantage of social forestry is that it involves the society and government at various levels in preservation of the vegetative cover, which is the most successful way to attempt afforestation. In Gujarat a phenomenally successful afforestation programme has been carried out by providing the schoolchildren with the seeds of the subabul tree, and encouraging them to look after their trees, which in turn supply the community with fuel and fodder. The effect of social forestry programmes in India has been discussed in detail by Agarwal and Narain in their edited volume, *The State of India's Environment 1984–85*.

but since then Nigeria has been importing timber. World Resources Institute in 1985 submitted a plan for arresting the destruction of the tropical forests (table 2.1) and stressed that current trends in deforestation cannot be reversed solely by forestry, but only with combined efforts from the agriculture, energy, and other sectors. Furthermore, the attempts have to involve local community groups, national and provincial governments, and the development assistance agencies. A five-year attempt at improving the condition of the tropical forests would require US$8,000, according to the submitted plan.

Table 2.1   Proposals for accelerated improvement in tropical forests

1   Improved fuelwood and agroforestry.
2   Proper land management on upland watersheds.
3   Improved forestry management for industrial use involving protection and management of natural forest, more intensive use of existing resources, accelerated industrial reforestation.
4   Conservation of tropical forest ecosystem by better government commitments and development agencies and strengthening of appropriate government agencies.
5   Strengthening of the institutions for research, training, and extension of services to the local community.

Source: World Resources Institute (1985) *Tropical Forests: Call for Action*, Washington, DC

It is also necessary to raise the awareness level of people away from the forested lands to the value of investment in their conservation. Important decisions about the future of the forests are taken in cities. Participation at various levels of the community is crucial for proper management practices which would allow use of the forest without extensive environmental degradation. An example of conservation at the international agency level would be the Man and the Biosphere Programme (MAB) of UNESCO which establishes Biosphere Reserves – multiple-use conservation areas that include both areas that are unaltered and areas that are modified by human activities. Such reserves serve as areas of study on tropical ecosystems. At a different level of conservation is the *Chipko* movement of India, where local villages have prevented destruction of natural vegetation by hugging the trees as they were about to be logged by outside business concerns, and thereby attracting public attention to the cause of preservation. The Kuna Indians on the offshore islands of Panama, indigenous people of the tropical rainforest, successfully maintained their traditional values in spite of outside pressure for development, and have established a wildlife reserve with research facilities for visiting scientists on part of their land.

Case study B

Changes in the Amazon rainforest

The 5.9 million km^2 Amazon Basin occupies over a third of South America. Most of it is in Brazil, but the headwaters of the Amazon drain large areas of the Andean states of Bolivia, Peru, Ecuador, Colombia, and Venezuela. In general, most of the Amazon Basin is under high rainforest (figure B.1) on acid soils from which nutrients have been washed out. Unlike other rainforest areas, the soils of the Amazon forest are low in nutrients even when a tree cover exists. The forest receives its nutrients from a network of fine roots found at the soil surface, which is mixed with organic material. The roots pick up nutrients directly from the decomposed litter, and nutrients do not get into the soil in any significant quantity. The traditional inhabitants have been various small groups of Amazonian Indians such as Yanomami, who live off the forest, without creating any significant environmental stress.

Figure B.1   The Amazon Basin

Case study B (*continued*)

To Brazil, trying to develop its resources, the sparcely populated forested vastness of the Amazon Basin is a great temptation. The forest contains large amounts of commercial timber and other forest products. It was rubber growing naturally (the plant *Hevea braziliensis*) that prompted the first large-scale alteration of the Amazon forest in the late nineteenth century. The cleared land attracts migrating peasantry. The mineral deposits of the area are considerable, including large deposits of iron and manganese. The iron reserves of Carajas, south of Belem, have attracted large-scale mining. Forest-based industries have been set up, and recently large tracts have been cleared for cattle ranching. The Brazilian government, poor migrating farmers, and large business organizations, including multi-nationals, have been involved in the development of the Amazon Basin.

Very few of the projects have been successful, and certainly none has been implemented without grave environmental consequences. The two early attempts to develop the interior of the Amazon – the gathering of natural rubber about a hundred years ago, and Henry Ford's attempt to establish a rubber plantation between the mid-1920s and 1945 – both failed. Examples of recent large-scale projects include a number of foreign involvements, such as the US shipping executive Daniel Ludwig's timber, wood pulp, and agriculture project at Jari over an area of 16,000 km². Such projects, often with government support at least at the beginning, have not always been successful, but usually have destroyed a large part of the rainforest, turned the land barren, and increased erosion.

The building of Trans-Amazon Highway and a connecting road network leading from the east into the Amazon Basin has been followed by migration of poor farmers into Rondônia and Acre (figure B.1). This has not been a successful migration in general, due to the difficulty in cultivating the soils of the Amazon tropical forest, and has often given rise to a sequence of forest destruction, soil erosion, and a further migration by the disappointed peasantry.

The results of such alterations are perceived at two levels: regional and global. The cleared areas of the Amazon rainforest suffer from soil infertility, erosion, and possible increase in flooding. The global effects have the potential to be extremely serious.

The Amazon carries about 20 per cent of the total river discharge in the world to the sea. Large-scale deforestation in the basin will ultimately alter the Amazon's discharge regime and sediment transport pattern. Changes at

Case study B (*continued*)

that level may have grave environmental consequences, and probable significant climatic changes have been predicted.

Another possible type of climatic modification is due to the destruction of the huge vegetation cover leading to a build-up of carbon dioxide in the atmosphere, which in turn would block the escape of terrestrial heat and raise the surface temperature. This would cause the melting of ice sheets raising the sea level, and ultimately leading to the inundation of low coastal cities. However, it should be stated that this chain of events has not yet been established clearly, especially the effect of extra carbon dioxide in the atmosphere. Another aspect of the global disaster would be the deplorable destruction of the vast number of species (both flora and fauna) that the Amazon rainforest holds.

It is of interest to note that recently the World Bank has been criticized for financially supporting the Brazilian Northwest Region Integrated Development Program (Polonoroeste), a development project connected with highway construction through the rainforest, which unfortunately resulted in rapid deforestation and uncontrolled migration.

Key ideas

1   Only a part of the original natural vegetation has survived in the Third World.
2   The three major areas of surviving tropical rainforests are the Amazon Basin, Equatorial Africa, and south and south-east Asia.
3   The rainforests should be perceived as storehouses of resources.
4   The tropical vegetation is disappearing rapidly to meet the demand for timber, fuelwood, and new agricultural land.
5   Fuelwood is an important source of energy in the Third World.
6   Forests have been replaced by plantations or cattle ranches in various parts of the tropics.
7   The effects of the deforestation, depending on the scale, could be local or global.
8   The management of the tropical forests should be carried out simultaneously at various levels: international, national, and local.

3
The environmental impact of land development

The background

Land development, especially extension of farming areas, happens mostly in response to a rise in population or a rising demand for a particular crop (plate 3.1). Pressure on land is created when the area concerned is expected to support more than the optimal number of people. It is not only the population size that creates pressure on land but also the crowding of people in the more advantageous geographical areas within a country and by the migration of less fortunate people to marginal areas in search of agricultural land. Even countries with an overall low population may end up with high density in certain regions. For example the concentration of the rural population of Venezuela is along the Andean foothills, not on the lower plains or the southern uplands. The population in western Malaysia is distributed along the two coastal plains, avoiding the central mountains. Pressure on land is also created by external interests as is the case in the clearing of the Central American forest for raising hamburger-oriented livestock. In addition, large-scale agricultural developments, the creation of valley bottom water reservoirs, the spread of industries or of urban settlements, all can create pressure on land by occupying the good agricultural land, and forcing a migration of the peasantry to other areas.

Whatever might be the underlying causes, agricultural expansion involves the settling and farming of marginal lands: areas which are difficult to cultivate and which would not be the first choice of most rural communities. The marginality is displayed in steep slopes, low rainfall, poor soils, and so on. It is a fragile environment which is very easily disturbed. Farming of such lands results in desertification, accelerated slope failures, soil erosion, and exhaustion. Interestingly the problems created by the misuse of land and their solutions are not necessarily all physical. In many cases a socio-economic appendage to the physical solution is needed. The application of technological solutions to ecological problems has to take into account the historical or cultural background of the people concerned, in order to persuade the people to utilize the land properly.

Case study C

Land degradation in El Salvador

El Salvador is 20,000 km^2 of the volcano-studded mountainous backbone of Central America steeply sloping down to a narrow coastal plain by the Pacific Ocean. The population of 775,000 at the beginning of the century now exceeds 5 million. Such a dense population exerts a heavy ecological pressure in this predominantly agricultural country. At one time, about 90 per cent of El Salvador, especially the steep mountain country, was under tropical deciduous forest. Centuries of grazing, mining, charcoal burning, spread of plantations, and subsistence agriculture have destroyed the forest. Not surprisingly about three-quarters of El Salvador, especially the mountain slopes, are ravaged by accelerated erosion. Soil erosion on slopes is combined with filling of the river channels further down with the eroded material travelling downslope. Details of such degradation have been described by Eckholm in his book, *Losing Ground*.

The degradation of the environment is, however, not entirely due to the size of El Salvador's agricultural population. The pattern of land ownership contributed greatly to the ecological disaster. About half of El Salvador's land has been for a long time in the form of large estates called *latifundias* occupying the best lands (coastal plains, valley flats, basin floors, and mid-volcano slopes), growing coffee, sugarcane, and cotton for export. A very small part of El Salvador's good agricultural land, on the other hand, is fragmented into a large number of small plots of subsistence farmers, most small farmers being thus forced into marginal lands on steep slopes and low fertility soils, which they have to cultivate without proper fallowing practices in order to survive, starting a vicious circle of progressively degraded land.

Plate 3.1   Rice grown on steep slopes, north Sumatra

El Salvador is not a unique case. It is a typical example of a situation where the degraded landscape cannot be recovered solely by technical solutions of reforestation, conservation measures, river control, and others. Further development of an export-oriented economy could very well worsen the problem by forcing even greater use of land as large plantations. Part of the solution has to come from a modification of agricultural practices and land tenure system. Population control, so important towards preventing environmental degradation, has very little chance of being effective unless the poor farmers are assured of a better socio-economic existence. The profits from commercial agriculture, which improve the Gross National Product statistics of a country, are seldom used to improve the environment or the fate of subsistence farmers. A landless tenant farmer or a subsistence farmer, perpetually under the threat of malnutrition affecting his family, cannot be expected to be always concerned about the degradation of the cnvironment. A government interested in protecting the national environment must communicate successfully the notion of the impending ecological disaster across a wide spectrum of people from the farmers to the politicians and bureaucrats.

Agricultural development: the general case

Agriculture in the Third World has supported a very large number of people for a very long time (plate 3.2). The traditional agricultural systems include shifting cultivation in the forests, sedentary farming in fertile regions (flood plains, coastal plains, volcanic slopes), irrigated farming in subhumid areas, and grazing of livestock in drier or uncultivable tracts. With the rise in population in recent years, traditional agricultural techniques have become insufficient to meet the demand for food in many places. As a result various modifications of the traditional system have taken place, not always without ecological problems.

Plate 3.2   Rice and coconut farming, Bali

The surviving tropical rainforests of South and Central America, Central Africa, and south and south-east Asia still cover a large area. The luxuriance of these forests perpetuates the myth that the tropical lands are indigenously fertile. Due to the efficient leaching of the soil, the tropical lands are productive only where the fertile constituents of the soil are regularly renewed either by decomposing leaves and branches on the forest floor, or by repeated flood alluviation on riverine plains, or by formation of virgin soils on fresh volcanic slopes. The traditional agriculture in the rainforest has been shifting cultivation practised by a small number of forest-dwellers, where a patch of land is cleared, burnt, and cultivated for a few years, and then abandoned following the drop in fertility and the proliferation of weeds. Usually the system implies a return to the abandoned plots in a number of years after renewed forest growth, and this system is able to support only a limited number of practitioners. Where such constraints can be met the system is ecologically sound, and land degradation is limited. An increase in population or a desire for greater material prosperity requires a return to old plots before the soil has had time to recover, with disastrous consequences in falling yield, general malnutrition, and increased soil erosion. The soils of the tropical rainforest can be cultivated continuously only with massive doses of fertilizers. In addition, due to the general intensity of the tropical rain, any land not under natural vegetation or crops is rapidly eroded by surface runoff, rills, and gullies. Many of the Third World countries have a colonial past; history is full of the failures of colonial masters who tried to impose a system of continuous cultivation on the soils of the cleared rainforest.

Even in the areas that are naturally fertile or where animal manure has been carefully used, as in the highlands of East Africa, the population density is causing too much pressure on the environment, leading to soil erosion and increased flooding in rivers. Spectacular effects of erosion are seen in Madagascar where heavy rains fall on steep slopes from which vegetation has been cleared. Even the ecologically stable system of the production of irrigated rice in the wet fields of Asia is under pressure, as in the Ganga Valley of India or on the island of Java in Indonesia. The solution to this problem arrived in the late 1960s and early 1970s in the form of an agricultural practice known as the Green Revolution. The Green Revolution is the result of decades of painstaking genetic research on various kinds of crops in several outstanding research projects such as Dr Norman Borlaug's wheat-breeding programme in Mexico or work in the International Rice Research Institute in the Philippines. In essence, the Green Revolution requires the use of improved high-yield varieties of cereals like wheat or rice grown with large inputs at appropriate times of fertilizer, water, and pesticide. The doubling or more of wheat and rice yields has enabled countries like Mexico, India, Pakistan, the Philippines, and Turkey to meet the demands of increasing population. There has been a phenomenal increase in world grain output from the 1960s onwards, and a very large part of it is due to the Green Revolution.

Certain environmental problems, however, may arise from this type of development. First, it is easier for the more prosperous farmers to take advantage of the Green Revolution, thereby increasing the disparity of wealth among the members of the community, which may or may not have a physical manifestation. Second, the fertilizers and pesticides used wash off the fields to pollute rivers or lakes, or leach into the subsurface to lower the quality of the groundwater. Third, both fertilizer production and irrigation require energy, and the rise in the price of oil and natural gas since 1973 has made energy a much more expensive commodity. Last, there may be biological complications such as genetic resistance to pesticides developed by various insects, or possible reduction of genetic diversity in crops. But on the whole, the Green Revolution has been successful, even if it has only bought time for the planners of population control.

Agricultural development: the marginal lands

The degradation of the environment as a result of agricultural expansion is, as expected, strongest in marginal lands. The expansion is of course connected with large increases in population and inequitable land tenure systems. There are three major types of marginal lands where such expansion takes place: areas where agriculture is possible with irrigation, drier areas with limited potential for crop growing but where grazing is possible, and areas of steep slopes with a very high erosion potential.

Agricultural development with irrigation in sub-humid areas

Land has been successfully cultivated under irrigation for thousands of years. The general practice of putting a barrier across a river to pond water and then redistributing the stored amount to agricultural fields via a network of canals is found throughout history, especially in subhumid/semi-arid areas like the Tigris-Euphrates Valley or the coastal desert area of Peru. Both in earlier times and recent years, a network of earth canals and waterlogged fields have led to seepage underground and a subsequent rise of the water table in semi-arid regions. When saline groundwater, as is found in these areas, rises to within a few metres of the surface, capillary action brings it to the surface itself, where the water evaporates leaving behind a layer of salt. Where this phenomenon is advanced, entire areas are covered with glistening white salt. In order to prevent such a condition, irrigation in subhumid areas should be planned concomitantly with provisions for better drainage so that waterlogging of the fields does not occur, and the canals should be lined with bricks or concrete.

The list of countries affected by salinity caused by the spread of irrigation water is extensive. In the Third World it includes the drier parts of India, Pakistan, Iraq, Iran, Syria, Jordan, other countries of western Asia, Peru, Argentina, north-east Brazil, and Mexico. Sometimes salinity is exacerbated by the human hand as in the Colorado Delta. The water that flows down the Colorado River from the USA to Mexico is highly saline due not only to the local geology, but also to the increased diversion of the water for agricultural use and its subsequent return to the river. The evaporative loss of part of the irrigated water in transit makes the remainder even more saline. Conditions worsened in 1961 when a piping programme started in Arizona, resulting in an increased salt content of the river water reaching Mexico. Finally, an agreement was reached between the two countries in 1973, by which the USA agreed to build a desalinization plant to lower the salt content of the water draining to Mexico. The spread of irrigation in subhumid areas requires simultaneous improvement in drainage conditions to prevent the accumulation of water in the fields. India is currently involved in the huge scheme of the Rajasthan Canal to turn a vast area of the Thar Desert and its fringes into productive agricultural land, and the effect of the drainage of the irrigated areas has to be carefully monitored.

The drier lands

About a third of the world is classified as desert of various types and degree, all of which have limited agricultural potential. Around the fringes of the major deserts, such as the Sahara or Atacama, there is usually a transitional belt which will support nomadic herdsmen in years of good rainfall. At other times, the fringes are too inhospitable even for that. The Sahel of Africa is such a fringe where years of drought bring starvation and famine to the people of Mauritania, Senegal, Mali, Burkina Faso, Niger, and Chad. Since the 1970s this has been disastrous enough to attract the attention of the world periodically (figure 3.1). In recent years there have been two periods of disastrous drought in Africa: 1968–73 and 1982–4. Over 100,000 people and a very large proportion of the livestock died in the Sahel in the famine of the early 1970s.

Beyond the Sahelian type of desert fringe lies a semi-arid environment, which is climatologically less hostile. Such an environment is found in part of all the west African countries listed above, and also in Sudan, Somalia, Ethiopia, Kenya, Tanzania, and in parts of Southern Africa, especially Botswana. In central and western Asia it includes the countries from Israel to Pakistan, the Thar of India; and in South America parts of Argentina and northern Chile. Much of this area has been supporting more than the optimal number of people and grazing animals. This has resulted in the destruction of natural vegetation, overgrazing, burning, and careless farming leading to the erosion of the landscape, windblown sand, salinization, and finally to a dry desert-like land. This process is called desertification.

It has been roughly estimated that desertification of our planet has affected collectively an area larger than Brazil, and is a primary mechanism for the spread of desert in our time. Desertification is helped by the strong rainfall variability in these areas, and the occasional pattern of dry years

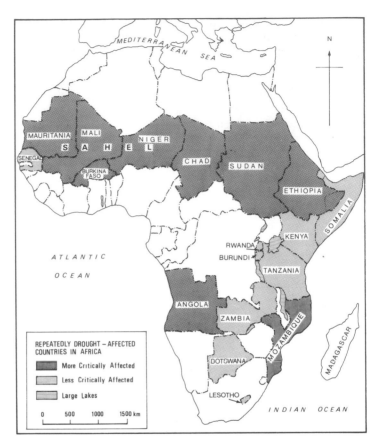

Figure 3.1   Drought-affected countries in Africa [Based on M.H. Glantz and R.W. Katz (1985) 'Drought as a constraint to development in sub-Saharan Africa', *Ambio* 14(6), 334–9]

tending to run together. A population of humans and grazing animals that is not a pressure on land during wet years becomes insupportable during such a dry spell. The desertification in the Sahel has also been accelerated by overgrazing and emphasis on cash crops such as cotton, groundnuts, and soyabeans in colonial times replacing food crops. The control of human and animal population, the restriction of human and animal migration to such areas, and judicious farming practices including controlled grazing may prevent desertification. Recovery of such degraded areas might be possible with large-scale afforestation as has been attempted in Algeria, carefully planned irrigation projects, and use of new cropping systems that maximize the vegetation cover on land. One should remember that the areas currently under desertification have supported a number of people for thousands of years, though the climate may have been kinder in the past.

The areas of steep slopes

Agricultural expansion on hillslopes usually ends in intensive erosion of the slope materials, and transportation of the sediment downslope to the streams at the bottom of the valleys. There the sediment raises the river beds, chokes the channels, and increases the potential for flooding. The effect of deforestation followed by agricultural expansion is easily seen when the sediment loads of streams in forested catchment areas and in cultivated ones are compared. The erosion occurs via various means: slope wash, gullies, and mass movements like debris slide or debris flow. Even the standard soil conservation techniques of cultivating on the terraces on hillslopes or contour fencing might not be sufficient to prevent slope degradation. Only large-scale afforestation of the slopes seems to be effective against erosion.

The speed of degradation is usually high, but certain areas like the Himalayas, the Andes, or parts of the East African Highlands are being eroded at an even higher rate because of the local geology, relief, and the nature of intense rainfall over the slopes. Java's irrigation systems have been clogged by sediment derived from erosion-prone mountain slopes. The highlands of Ethiopia are being heavily eroded as demonstrated by the sediment load of the Blue Nile. The combination of bare mountain terrain and population pressure (Ethiopia is the third most populous country in Africa) results in a landscape of bare subsistence and famine, desolation and impending disaster, with sediment-laden rivers shifting their courses at the bottom. A similar pattern of land degradation arising out of population pressure is found on the Andean slopes of Bolivia, Peru, and Venezuela. Studies in Colombia show an acceleration of slope erosion, landslides, and valley bottom sedimentation in similar fashion.

Perhaps the best studied and most spectacular examples come from the Himalayas, where a combination of local geology, steep slopes on high mountains, and intense monsoon rainfall disastrously expose the folly of deforestation, overgrazing, and cultivation of steep marginal lands. The catchment of the Kosi River, draining out of the high eastern Himalayas and one of the most spectacular basins of the world, has also been described as one of the most eroded ones in the world. Similarly misuse of land in the upper Indus Valley of Pakistan releases enormous quantities of sediment which has effectively shortened the life of the huge Mangla and Tarbela reservoirs. Such lowering of the life expectancy of reservoirs due to bad land-use practices has been reported from many countries including some in the First World. Both agricultural expansion and grazing have led to deforestation and subsequent erosion of the Himalayan slopes.

Other types of land degradation

Other types of land degradation problems may locally assume disastrous proportions. The formation of badlands in semi-arid areas via the development of gully networks, or the despoiling of the landscape by mining, are two such examples. A very large part of the Chambal Valley of central India is being rapidly eroded by a spreading network of gullies and streams known locally as ravines.

Mining activities degrade the landscape by laying barren the land and opening the huge chasms of opencast mining; by polluting the water from drainage of mined materials; by denuding forests both through direct deforestation and by releasing pollutants in the air that cause acid rain; or by choking the landscape by a layer of dust that settles on the agricultural fields. In the USA, for example, a reclamation plan has to be filed and approved by government before mining for coal can begin. Such practices should be followed in spite of the lure of economic development based on extraction of coal and minerals in a less developed country.

The rivers and coasts of the Third World exhibit too many cases of sediment being released in the waters. The results may be limited due to the dilution involved, but one wonders about the effect on neighbouring mangrove assemblages or coral reefs. The development of land should be planned so that the impact of deforestation, agricultural expansion, and mining are minimized. This can be achieved only by a combination of technical, social, and economic solutions. Crop management, soil conservation measures, and simultaneous establishment of irrigation and drainage have a higher rate of success when they arrive with population control and land reforms.

Case study D

The Yallahs Valley, Eastern Jamaica: an example of utilization of marginal lands

Eastern Jamaica is a land with a deeply dissected mountainous centre surrounded by narrow coastal plains. The 37-km-long Yallahs river drains 163 km^2 of the southern slopes of the central Blue Mountains (plate D.1) into a basin with the impressive and persistent local relief of 450–600 m, with steep slopes at angles of 20°–30°. Extensive landslides and faulting also help to maintain this landscape. The annual rainfall increases from 1,500 mm near the mouth of the Yallahs river on the southern coast to more than 2,500 mm in the north over the upper Yallahs Basin. There is a seasonal component in the rainfall, December to April being the dry season. Some of the rainfall arrives in the form of violent intense showers, at times from tropical storms that occasionally reach hurricane force when rainfall of nearly 250 mm a day is not rare. The soils are thin, full of pebbles, not

Plate D.1   The Yallahs River, Jamaica

Case study D (*continued*)

particularly fertile, and heavily eroded by mass movement, slope wash, and gullies.

An export-oriented agriculture resulting in the cultivation of sugarcane, coffee, tobacco, cotton, and cinchona has replaced most of the natural luxuriant forest vegetation over the last 400 years. This used to be plantation agriculture in large estates, with slave labour, which mainly produced sugarcane, and higher up in the mountains, coffee or cinchona. A large number of plantations were abandoned in the mid-nineteenth century due to the emancipation of slaves in 1838 and the abolition of the tariff protection of the Jamaican sugar in the British market. Coffee plantations were abandoned about the same time. By the second half of the nineteenth century, slopes that had been cleared were either utilized for plantation or subsistence agriculture, or were allowed to develop a secondary growth of grasslands and thorn trees, locally known as the *ruinate* lands. Another spell of land clearing happened towards the end of the nineteenth century when cultivation of bananas both in small holdings and plantations became commercially viable in Jamaica.

The spread of agriculture due to population pressure was remarkable, particularly considering the minute size of the holdings, the infertility of the soils, and the steepness of the slopes where even terracing is not carried out and a fence of brushwood tied together at the downslope end of the plots functions as the soil-protecting device instead. In the Yallahs Valley, human endeavours arising out of population pressure have speeded up the already rapid process of erosion.

At present, most of the Yallahs Valley slopes are under *ruinate* bush, strip cultivation, or pasture with some forests and afforestation attempts. The general picture is that of smallholdings with vegetables, fruit trees, and pasture with some coffee on the upper slopes. The Yallahs Valley Land Authority is responsible for planning and monitoring the use of the land, but it is difficult to utilize a landscape such as this (plate D.2) without

Key ideas

1   Pressure on land is created by many factors: high population density, non-uniform population distribution, skewed distribution of the size of land holdings, and large-scale development projects.

2   The Green Revolution has been very successful in increasing crop production in some countries.

Case study D (*continued*)

Plate D.2   The eroded hillslopes in the Yallahs Basin

creating extreme erosion on slopes and floodprone rivers at the bottom of the valley. It is interesting to note that the land capability map of Jamaica lists the almost entire basin as either not, or marginally, suitable for cultivation and recommends that it remains under natural vegetation, or tree crops or pasture.

3   Agricultural expansion to marginal areas has to cope with two types of problems: shortage of water and erosion of land.
4   Extension of irrigation without drainage into dry areas may result in salinization of the land.
5   Extreme care should be taken in utilizing mountain slopes.
6   The problems of land degradation that arise from agricultural expansion require technical, social, and economic solutions – all three.

4
Development of water resources

The hydrological background

Nature manages her water resources extremely efficiently with techniques for self-purification and for managing on a finite budget by recirculation of moisture. The recirculation technique is known as the hydrologic cycle, which is best explained diagrammatically (figure 4.1). About 97 per cent of earth's water is stored in the oceans in a saline form. Almost the entire amount of freshwater is locked frozen in Antarctica and Greenland. A significant amount of the remainder lies at a considerable depth in the subsurface. The water that is normally available to us comes from the atmosphere, the land surface, and the shallow subsurface, and constitutes an extremely small part of the total world inventory. Technologically it is feasible to acquire, process, and utilize water from the oceans, ice sheets, and deep underground, but the cost makes such efforts uneconomic. One of the favourite expressions in hydrology textbooks is that people expect water to be cheaper than dirt.

Part of the precipitation is interrupted by the vegetation, and is either evaporated back to the atmosphere or runs down the plant stems or trunks to reach the ground. The water that reaches the ground surface enters into the soil (infiltration), or fits small (1–2 cm deep) surface depressions, and, if the rain is intense, starts to flow on the surface (surface runoff) to rills and gullies, and ultimately to larger streams. The water that has infiltrated into the soil fills the smaller pores in it, and drains downwards by gravity via the larger pores to the groundwater below. Most of the water stored in the soil

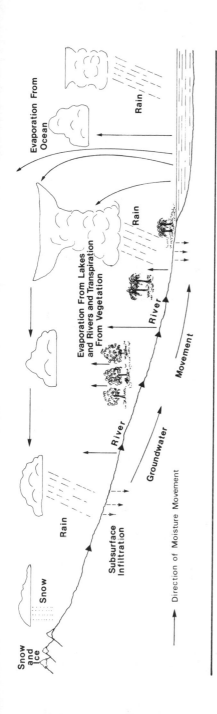

Figure 4.1 The hydrologic cycle and the water storage [Figures in percentage taken from R.G. Barry (1969) 'The world hydrologic cycle', in R.J. Chorley (ed.) *Water, Earth and Man*, London, Methuen]

(soil moisture) is available to plants via their root systems. The groundwater table is raised by gravity drainage, which accelerates the lateral flow of the subsurface water to wells and streams. The amount of water which will go via the different paths of this system is determined by local conditions and varies seasonally. Any development that alters the local environment alters the paths, and thereby the available amount and quality of the water supply. Clearing of land or urbanization increases surface runoff and the potential for floods in nearby streams. Afforestation, on the other hand, increases both interception and infiltration, and is expected to reduce floods and increase groundwater flow in the subsurface. Any water management scheme redistributes the amount of water along the various paths of the system, some of the results of which could be undesirable.

The story of large-scale management of water goes back at least 6,000 years. Structures for storing water behind dams and for distributing stored water have been associated with ancient civilizations in various parts of the world: Egypt, western Asia, India, and China. Some rivers, like the Nile or the Tigris-Euphrates, have long histories of water utilization. At present, demand for water has risen to a very high level due to the general increase in the world population and the per capita increase in water usage concomitant with a developing economy. Certain types of water use are consumptive, while water from other uses can be reutilized after purification. Table 4.1 describes the major uses of water.

Table 4.1   Types of water use

Type of use	Characteristics
Municipal: potable water	Consumptive.
Municipal: other uses	Usually heavily polluted after use. Possibility of reuse after proper treatment.
Industrial	Various uses, a large proportion for cooling purposes. Level of pollution depends on industry involved. Substantial portion could be reused after treatment.
Hydro-electricity generation	Almost entirely reusable. Some evaporation loss from reservoirs.
Agriculture	Polluted by fertilizers, pesticides, and saline concentration. Could be reused under favourable conditions after treatment. Otherwise usually ends up in local streams.
Navigation	All reusable. Level of pollution low.
Recreation	Reusable. Level of pollution low. Some pathogenic organisms might be present.
Propagation of fish and wildlife	Reusable. Level of pollution low.

As countries develop, not only does the total demand rise, but also the relative importance of various types of use changes. The supply to meet this demand could be from rivers, lakes, or groundwater, depending on local conditions. For example in relatively less humid areas, groundwater becomes an important source of supply. The growth of a large city often requires large-scale groundwater extraction, or water has to be piped in from a source many kilometres away.

The attempt to meet the extra demands for water of a specific standard that arise out of progressive development could be difficult and costly, and may result in large-scale endeavours leading to environmental degradation. For example in recent years huge dams and reservoirs have been built which are associated with certain ecological problems (case study E). There are several 300-km-long reservoirs in Africa: Lake Volta behind the Akosombo Dam, Lake Kariba behind the Kariba Dam, and Lake Nasser behind the Aswan High Dam. Case study F indicates the level at which the water of one of the world's largest rivers has been degraded by the sheer size of the demand for water for various purposes. The development of water resources carries with it the onus of careful planning and its implementation. The planning should go beyond the engineering feasibility study, and should examine the possible impact of the development on the environment, wildlife, and society.

In the rest of the chapter some of the areas where problems might arise as a result of utilization of water resources in order to meet the increasing demand are discussed. The examples have been taken from three areas: the problem of water supply to settlements, the pollution of water due to population pressure, and the need for environmental planning for large-scale water utilization projects.

The supply of water to settlements

About ten years ago the World Health Organisation carried out a survey on the access to drinking water in the developing world. As expected, there was a great disparity in the availability of potable water between the urban and rural sectors. Only 20 per cent of the rural community (248 million) had access to potable water, a figure that rose to 390 million and 75 per cent in the urban areas. These overall figures hide huge disparities which are revealed when the data are broken down into smaller areas: figures ranged from 100 per cent in some urban settlements to less than 1 per cent in certain rural areas. The numbers have risen in the last ten years, but large areas of the Third World are still without safe drinking water or proper sanitary arrangement which prevents the pollution of water sources.

One of the better results of development has been the associated arrival of potable water which reduces health hazards. The diseases associated with

Case study E

The Aswan Dam on the Nile

The 6,695-km-long Nile has the longest known history of water utilization (about 7,000 years) and as a result the longest record of flow in the world. The water has been utilized for basin irrigation from the passage of annual floods for thousands of years, and from the early nineteenth century a number of barrages have been built across the river.

The Nile has two major sources (figure E.1): the White Nile, whose headwaters rise in Equatorial Africa beyond Lake Victoria, and the Blue Nile, which has its source in Lake Tana in the Ethiopian highlands. The flow of the White Nile headwaters is well regulated by several lakes and the vast Sudd swamps of southern Sudan. The Blue Nile, however, is an extremely floodprone seasonal stream, and along with its major tributary, the Atbara, brings down the sediment-laden annual flood of Egypt. The flood sediment, deposited over the floodplains and delta lands of Egypt, has made the lower Nile Valley an exceptionally fertile and populated area.

In the twentieth century several dams have been built across the White and Blue Nile, each with certain beneficial contributions and some environmental problems. The biggest of the Nile dams is the Aswan High Dam, built in 1971 with Soviet assistance. It is a huge structure with a large reservoir behind it (Lake Nasser), the tail end of which stretches into Sudan. The showpiece engineering project has increased Egypt's potential arable land from 2.8 million to 3.6 million ha, and has been instrumental in creating and maintaining self-sufficiency in wheat and export of rice. The planned annual capacity of hydro-electricity is 10,000 million kilowatts. Agricultural areas have been converted from basin irrigation dependent on seasonal flooding to perennial irrigation, and flood control measures have improved. Unfortunately the project simultaneously caused some environmental degradation.

As might be expected from its location, Lake Nasser has a very high evaporation rate, which reduces its efficiency. The sedimentation rate is also high, and that not only reduces storage capacity, but more importantly it prevents the fertile silt from reaching the agricultural areas downstream of the dam forcing the cultivators to be dependent on fertilizers. The lack of water and sediment reaching the Mediterranean via the lower Nile has resulted in coastal erosion in the delta and saltwater intrusion. The lack of nutrients reaching the Mediterranean has destroyed the rich sardine fishery offshore, which is partially compensated for by fishing in Lake Nasser. Even more disastrous has been the spread of schistosomiasis in the irrigated areas and salinization of part of the irrigated land.

Case study E (*continued*)

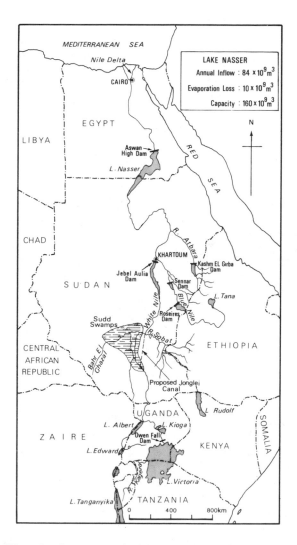

Figure E.1   Water development projects in the Nile Basin [Based on D. Hammerton (1972) 'The Nile River – a case history', in R.T. Oglesby, C.A. Carlson, and J.A. McCann (eds) *River Ecology and Man*, New York, Academic Press]

unsatisfactory water supply are various types of gastro-enteritic diseases, such as cholera, typhoid, amoebic and bacillary dysentery, infectious hepatitis, and so on. Other diseases, such as schistosomiasis, onchocerciasis (river blindness), trypanosomiasis (sleeping sickness), and guinea worm could be endemic where people have to go to a water course for their supply. Schistosomiasis, unfortunately, may increase with the development of water resources, primarily by the spread of irrigation canals and ditches. This leads to the extension and year-round establishment of the habitat of snails which act as hosts to the schistosomiasis parasite. The spread of schistosomiasis with stable perennial irrigation systems has been noticed in Egypt, Sudan, Kenya, and the Transvaal, where the infection rate in the irrigated European farms was nearly 70 per cent above that of drier reservations. In the irrigated parts of Kenya, 100 per cent infection rates have been noticed among schoolchildren. In the heavily infected areas of Egypt, the male and female life expectancy in the 1970s was 27 and 25 years respectively. Unless precautions are taken, year-round water availability also leads to increased incidences of mosquito-borne diseases: malaria, filaria, yellow fever, or arborivorous encephalitides. These details are taken from a summary of the survey by Biswas.

Apart from the improvement in health, bringing drinking water to the user is extremely beneficial to the women of rural areas. In the Third World it is not unknown for village women to walk several hours a day to fetch water. The bringing of safe drinking water to the user frees the women from this burden, and not only provides time for productive work but also decreases the physical stress on the relatively less-nourished women members of the family, who tend to consume less at meals, leaving most of the food for the men and children.

So far as the supply to the urban areas is concerned, ideally a city should have a safe drinking water supply, enough water at adequate pressure for fire-fighting, and water to meet the industrial demand of the area. This requires a source, a treatment system, and a distributory network. The requirements of a dependable water supply are twofold: ensuring the supply of water to meet the total demand, and maintaining the quality of the water needed to meet the various types of specific demand within the total. The volume of water required by an urban settlement depends on the population, the ambient standard of living, the climate, and the demand from industries.

However, many cities of the Third World have become extremely crowded with development and the associated better job prospects than those found in the rural areas. A number of city-dwellers are forced to live in unsatisfactory conditions with little or no access to properly treated water or sanitary facilities. This leads to contamination of water especially in the rainy season. The rapid spread of cities also results in widespread use of groundwater, which unless properly monitored may lead to environmental degradation. Shallow groundwater sources in urban areas with inadequate sanitary systems are often polluted. The growth of industries compound the problem by contaminating water supplies by various synthetic chemicals released from the plant as industrial effluent.

Pollution of the waterways

All types of development – agricultural, industrial, and settlement – create large amounts of detritus and polluted materials which then find their way to the channels draining the area. Given sufficient time, rivers may cleanse themselves of some of the polluted material, but if the population pressure in the valley is high, such undesirable effects of development tend to persist. The river simultaneously becomes the way of pollution disposal and the source of drinking water. Case study F on the Ganga River is an excellent example of this problem.

The types of pollution found in rivers and lakes with development, their sources, and the undesirable effects of such pollution are summarized in table 4.2. Rivers have their way of dealing with organic wastes. When organic wastes from urban or industrial effluents, or from agricultural fields, enter the stream, the bacteria and protozoa which are present in the water utilize them as food in the presence of dissolved oxygen in the water. This demand for oxygen for degradation of organic wastes is referred to as biochemical oxygen demand (BOD). It is used as a pollution measure, and calculated as the amount in mg of molecular oxygen required to process 1 litre of polluted water in this fashion. As oxygen is removed from the water for processing organic wastes, its amount in the river water drops, which is known as the oxygen sag (figure 4.2). Oxygen is then replenished from the atmosphere by a process known as reaeration, and, as the processing of organic wastes goes on, the demand for dissolved oxygen drops simultaneously. As a result the oxygen in the water comes back to the previous level, along with normal aquatic organisms. However, the replenishment of oxygen requires the water to travel over some distance, and the addition of polluted matter within this distance would be undesirable.

In general, regarding the municipal and industrial sources of pollution, it is desirable to treat the effluent to an acceptable level before discharging it into the river where it can be further diluted. Unfortunately this does not always happen. This problem is not restricted to the Third World, as many instances of irregular industrial discharge to the Rhine indicate. It is also possible to clean up a polluted river, as has been shown by the work on the Thames, but treatment is expensive and in the Third World the cleaning up of a river is not necessarily perceived as progressive in the same way as the

Case study F

The Ganga River in India: a case study of a river in use

The Ganga is 2,525 km long, and drains a 1 million km^2 basin (figure F.1). Over 80 per cent of the basin is in India, where it constitutes more than a quarter of India's total land area, and carries a quarter of its water resources. The river rises in the Himalayas from a glacier snout at 4,100 m elevation, but for most of its course, it flows through a vast alluvial plain at low elevations. The majority of the tributaries are both snowmelt and rainfed like the Ganga itself, although most of the south bank ones are

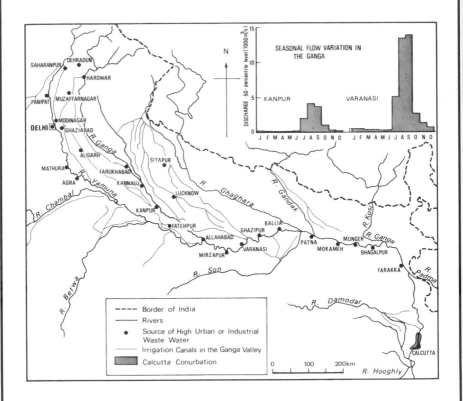

Figure F.1   The Ganga Valley

Case study F (*continued*)

entirely dependent on rainfall. Rainfall over the basin is controlled by the south-west monsoon, about 70 per cent of the annual rainfall arriving in four months (June–September). The river discharge thus shows considerable seasonal fluctuation.

Most of the basin, especially the part in the plains, is under agriculture. About 500,000 km^2 of the area is cultivated, some double or even triple cropped. Forests occupy only 14 per cent of the area against the desired norm of 33 per cent of the Indian national forest policy. Forest depletion is common even in the steep mountains of the upper basin. Considerable erosion of the basins and high sediment load in the stream are common especially at the beginning of the rainy season.

Approximately 240 million people (more than the population of the USA) live in the basin. The basin is highly rural, but still the urban population rises to nearly 40 million people in more than 600 towns and cities. The distribution of urban centres is uneven, being higher in parts of the upper Ganga Valley and at the lower end in West Bengal. A large number of urban settlements, some of considerable size (examples: Ghaziabad, 226,000; Aligarh, 200,000; Kanpur, 1.5 million; Allahabad, 590,000; Varanasi, 719,000; Patna, 623,000; Calcutta conurbation, about 10 million), are located directly on the banks of the Ganga. The water of the Ganga is used mainly for the following:

1 Irrigation – networks of canals take out large volumes of water to sustain agriculture in the valley. This leads to a drop in discharge for some distance below the canal headworks.
2 Domestic use – both urban and rural settlements use the river as a source for drinking water and other domestic uses including sewerage disposal.
3 Industrial use – the river supplies water to the industries located mainly in the urban areas of the valley, and especially in the two concentrations of urban settlements mentioned above. The industries on the bank include tanneries, petrochemical and fertilizer complexes, pesticide factories, rubber, jute, textile and paper mills, and distilleries.
4 Dispersal of waste water – waste water from agricultural fields, cities, and industries is released into the river, and not always with proper treatment.
5 Navigation.

Case study F (*continued*)

6   Religious practices – the water of the Ganga is holy to the Hindus and the river is extensively used for bathing. On certain holy days of the year, millions of pilgrims bathe at certain points along the river. The river is also used for disposal of human bodies for the same reason.

The nature of the physical environment and the high and various demands on the water lower the ambient quality of the river water. Untreated urban waste water is the prime polluter of the Ganga followed by industrial effluents. The untreated waste water arrives even from large cities like Varanasi, and such point sources of extreme pollution make the passage of the river through the states of Uttar Pradesh, Bihar, and West Bengal hazardous. The organic pollution from rural areas is widely distributed, and probably does not constitute a hazard except in very densely settled areas. The agricultural waste water also causes pollution problems, especially from fields with high applications of fertilizers and pesticides.

The problem of maintaining the quality of the water is accelerated during the low season, and also downstream of the points of water withdrawal for irrigation. The quality fluctuates depending on the density of population on banks, location of urban centres, and location of tributary junctions. For example in the reach between Kanauj and Kanpur, the BOD rises to the very high level of 10–20 mg/1. The colliform bacteria count is also rather high.

A regular programme for monitoring water quality in the Ganga was started in 1979. This involves sampling at various stations along the channel

building of an industrial plant. The limitation of resources and awareness, the low priority given to environmental protection, and the power of the industrial establishments determine that the pollution of waterways will continue.

Implementation of large-scale projects

The implementation of large-scale projects designed to improve the availability of water resources is an integral part of the planned development of the Third World countries. Multipurpose storage reservoirs constructed behind large dams impound water for irrigation, hydroelectricity generation, flood amelioration, municipal use, and recreation. A network of canals is

Case study F (*continued*)

at regular time intervals. In order to improve the general quality of the water of the river it is necessary to control the land use in the basin, the discharge of waste water effluents, and other intense uses of the river. An integrated plan and considerable effort and resources are necessary to achieve this, which is being worked out. Such problems as stated here are often accentuated as a result of development, for example higher use of pesticides, building of factories, and urban expansion, which tend to occur in large river valleys. A Pollution Control Research Institute has started in Ranipur, near Hardwar in the Himalayas. The Ganga clean-up project was officially launched by the Prime Minister, Rajiv Gandhi, in June 1986 at Varanasi. Financial and technological assistance are available from the UN Development Programme, Britain, the Netherlands, and France. There are some encouraging signs such as the formation of the local action groups like the Swatchh Ganga Abhijan of Varanasi, and the successful overhauling of the sewerage system of the holy town of Hardwar so that the bathing pilgrims are spared the upstream disposal of the town's waste water. The clearing up of the Ganga is a massive enterprise, and would involve among others treating the waste water of hundreds of cities and enforcing the river bank industries to treat their effluent much more stringently than ever before. Above all, the dwellers of the basin have to be involved. Non-government groups are being organized to ensure public participation in the massive clean-up campaign which, it is expected, will begin to be effective in a few years time.

spread to bring the water to demand areas. The projects, however, may give rise to certain types of environmental problems, especially if constructed without proper understanding of the regional conditions. Proper planning requires the availability of long-term hydrologic data, which is usually not available. Even short-term records of hydrologic, geomorphic, or biologic characteristics of the river basin concerned are often scarce. Though some of the gaps may be filled by synthetic hydrology or reconnaissance studies, the problem is not entirely solved, and the lack of information could have some unforeseen and unfortunate effects on the environment. Construction of dams, reservoirs, and canals should be viewed not only as engineering problems executed on the basis of decisions taken on grounds of economic or political expediency, but also as large-scale modifications of the

Table 4.2   Pollutants of water: types, sources, and effects

Type	Major sources	Effects
Oxygen-demanding wastes	Sewage (animal and human), industrial wastes (food processing plants, paper mills, oil refineries, tanning mills), runoff from agricultural lands, decaying vegetation.	Sag in dissolved oxygen, harmful effects on most aquatic organisms, foul odours.
Agents of infectious diseases	Untreated domestic sewage and animal wastes.	Spread of waterborne diseases, especially of gastro-enteritic tract, polio, infectious hepatitis.
Plant nutrients	Domestic sewage, industrial wastes, phosphorus from detergents, runoff from fertilized fields, fossil fuel combustion.	Algal blooms, excessive aquatic weeds, degraded taste and odour of water, oxygen depletion.
Synthetic organic compounds	Fuels, plastic, fibres, detergent, paints, pesticides, herbicides, food additives, etc.	Possible toxic effect to aquatic life, birds, and humans; possibility of genetic defects and cancer; algal blooms and aquatic weed growth; foul odour.
Inorganic chemicals and minerals	Mineral acids, inorganic salts, and finely divided metals or metal compounds, from mining and industry; petrol with lead, urban runoff.	Increases acidity, salinity, and toxicity of water often with disastrous effects.
Oil	Machines, vehicles, tanker spills, pipeline breaks, etc.	Disruption of ecosystems and aesthetic damage of the environment.
Sediments	Poor agricultural practice; destruction of forests; mining; construction activities.	Filling of channels and reservoirs; increase in turbidity of water; reduction of certain members of aquatic population.
Radioactive material	Natural sources, uranium mining, nuclear power generation, and weapon testing.	Cancer and genetic defects.
Heat	Cooling water released from industries and power plants.	Harmful effect on aquatic life, even fatal to some species; water solubility of oxygen decreased; increased chemical reactions.

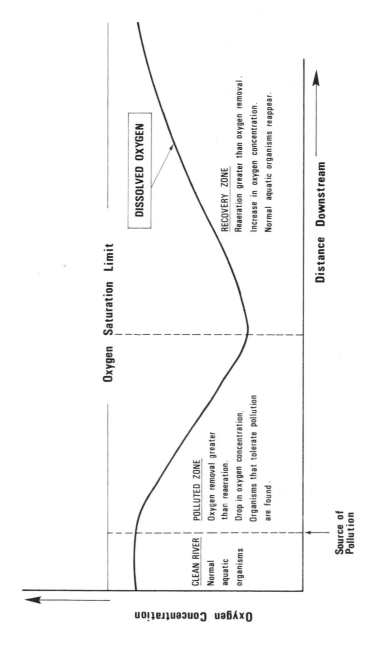

Figure 4.2 The oxygen sag curve

environment which may or may not have several undesirable side-effects.

If the catchment area is undergoing active degradation as a result of forest clearance, or the spread of agriculture, or if the natural conditions indicate a rapid rate of erosion resulting from regional geology, high relief and intense rainstorms, the derived sediment will arrive at the reservoir at a rapid rate leading to the lowering of its water-storage capacity. The upstream catchment area therefore requires careful land management. A considerable amount of sediment and water arrives in the river, not via the large tributaries, but through smaller streams and by surface wash. Land management over the entire watershed is therefore needed. If flood control is the prime objective, a number of small upstream reservoirs may be more effective than one large downstream one. If silting is a problem, the catchment should be left vegetated as far as possible.

The construction of a dam usually affects the channel downstream. The water released from the dam being low in sediment load has a tendency to erode and deepen the channel. The most commonly quoted example of this comes from the First World. After the completion of the Hoover Dam, the Colorado River degraded the channel below the dam extensively. The problem of the Colorado is common, and should be remembered at the planning stage because the lowering of the channel may result in difficulties with the intake of river water for various purposes. A different problem affects the stream courses where the tributaries contribute a large amount of sediment load. Dam closures and the subsequent decrease in the volume of water in the downstream channel result in the raising of the river bed. Downstream channel alteration depending on the nature of the environment may result in difficulties with water intake, or in channel shifting, or in increased flooding.

Another possible side-effect that should be taken into consideration at the planning stage is the drowning of valuable agricultural or residential land, or the possible inundation of areas of great natural beauty. Reservoirs in the uninhabited tropical rainforest may also drown the habitat of rare plants or animals. Dams may block the migratory paths of fish unless fish ladders are built at the damsite. Certain projects dramatically alter the environment, as was the case with the Aswan Dam.

The story of the Aswan High Dam and Lake Nasser illustrates many aspects of the implementation of a large-scale engineering project in the Third World. The project is often implemented with imported technology and financial assistance. There is insufficient ecological information for a proper environmental impact assessment to be made, and unlike the Nile, the hydrological data are usually not forthcoming. The project becomes a political showpiece, and unless there is environmental degradation of high order, such problems may be little recognized.

It is not suggested that large-scale engineering projects for river basin

.development be abandoned. What is implied is the need for prior investigation, especially concerning both possible environmental impact and the reliability of the project site. This general rule is of increased significance in the Third World, as often the background information so necessary for planning is very scanty, and political expediency requires a large engineering showpiece project which can be constructed with imported technology. The lack of information and local experience can be disastrous.

Key ideas

1 Demand for water increases directly with rise in population and with economic development.
2 Certain types of water use are consumptive, while water from other uses can be reutilized after treatment.
3 Large areas of the Third World are still without safe drinking water or proper sanitary arrangement. One of the best results of development is the arrival of safe drinking water which reduces health hazards.
4 Water is polluted from a variety of sources: human sewage, animal wastes, mining, industry, pesticides, fertilizers, detergents. Rivers are usually capable of purifying themselves of a limited amount of oxygen-demanding wastes.
5 Large-scale water development projects bring both benefits and environmental problems.
6 Background information and some local experience are necessary for successful planning of large-scale water development projects.

5
Development and changing air quality

The constituents of air

By air we refer to a mixture of gases that envelopes the surface of our planet. Remarkably the composition of this mixture is nearly constant from the ground level to a height of 80 km. The two major constituents of air are nitrogen (78 per cent by volume) and oxygen (approximately 21 per cent). Argon and carbon dioxide are also present but together they constitute only about 1 per cent. The remaining major constituent, water vapour, fluctuates between 0.01 and 5 per cent. A large number of gases, the minor constituents of air, make up about 0.01 per cent by volume. When some of these are present in sufficient quantity to affect the physical well-being of humans, animals, vegetation, and materials, they are considered pollutants of air. Such pollutants may exist as solid particles, as liquid droplets, in a gaseous state, or as a mixture; usually if air is polluted it is simultaneously by more than one kind of pollutant. Local concentrations of such pollutants, as often found in industrial and urban areas, are accentuated by meteorological (Figure 5.1) and topographic conditions which prevent the mixing of air and the associated dilution effects. This occurs, for example, in agglomerations such as Mexico City.

The spectre of air pollution hangs over industrial and urban centres. The air pollution over London in the 1950s, and several disastrous instances of pollution over New York in the 1950s and 1960s, are textbook examples. Both London and New York are now much cleaner as far as their air is concerned, due to concerted efforts put in after such disastrous episodes.

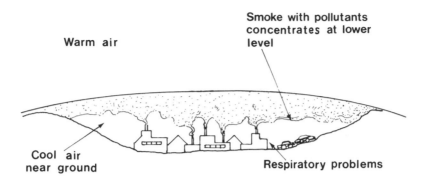

TEMPERATURE INVERSION IN A VALLEY

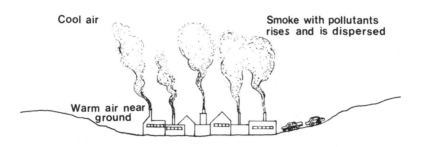

NORMAL CASE OF DROP IN TEMPERATURE UPWARDS

Figure 5.1   Inversion of temperature and air pollution

Unfortunately as the Third World countries go through industrial and urban development, such attempts to keep the air clean have not yet started to happen

The major pollutants of air are oxides of sulphur and nitrogen, carbon monoxide, hydrocarbons, photochemical oxidants (ozone, organic aldehydes, and peroxyacyl nitrates or PANs), and particulates. The major sources of pollutants are various modes of transportation, stationary fuel combustion, industry, and disposal of solid wastes. The concentration of the pollutants of air is measured as either parts per million by volume (ppm) or the mass of pollutants in microgrammes to the volume of containing air ($\mu g/m^3$). The details of the agents, sources, and effects of air pollution are listed in table 5.1.

Development in rural areas and air pollution

Air pollution in rural areas is mainly from the burning of natural vegetation and wind action on bare fields. Large-scale clearing of forests for agricultural expansion, especially by burning, may even result in temporary air pollution over nearby cities as sometimes happens in south-east Asia. In rural areas, if cooking is done over firewood in an enclosed space, it subjects the cook to an extremely high level of air pollution.

Mining, industrial activities, and air pollution

Particulates in concentrated form pervade the air in mining areas. The pollution is caused by blasting, which releases particulates and noxious fumes, and by wind blowing across open-cast mines, across waste heaps, and across open dumps of toxic mined products like asbestos. Extraction of mineral resources is an early and common stage in the development of the Third World countries, where safety rules and regulations are not always rigorously imposed.

Mine workers are expected to work in appalling conditions for long periods at very low pay. Safety measures are uncommon, and the incidence of accidents is high. Respiratory diseases and eye ailments are frequent. The clustering of stone quarries and crushers lead to a thick pall of silica dust over the region, prolonged inhalation of which may cause silicosis with irritant cough, shortness of breath, and chest pains. Agarwal and Narain have given some examples of such pollution and its effect from India. A survey of such an area near Delhi showed 17 per cent of the workers to be incurably affected. The dust impairs agriculture in the nearby fields as seen

Table 5.1 Air pollution: types, sources, effects, and controls

Type	Source	Effect	Controls
Sulphur oxides	Combustion of sulphur-bearing coal. Petroleum products. Industrial processes, particularly those involving smelting of sulphide-ores of copper, zinc, and lead.	Acid rain damages buildings and vegetation. Accelerated corrosion of materials. Affects the respiratory system. High concentration (10 ppm) causes eye and throat irritation.	Reduction in use of sulphur-bearing coal. Clearing of coal of some sulphur-compounds. Limestone injection in furnaces. Use of alkalized alumina.

Table 5.1 (*cont:*)

Type	Source	Effect	Controls
Nitrogen oxides: the two oxides are nitric oxide (NO) and nitrogen dioxide (NO$_2$)	Combustion of fossil fuels. Transportation.	NO$_2$ concentration in air affects respiratory tract.	
Particulates	Stationary combustion in households and power plants, especially those using coal. Motor vehicle emission. Refuse incineration. Burning of vegetation. Industry such as blast furnaces and smelters.	Respiratory diseases; possibility of lung and stomach cancer, especially if toxic material is present in particulate form. Particulates between 0.1 to 5 μm most likely to affect humans. Loss of visibility. Increases the effect of other pollutants.	Less use of coal for power generation. Location of power plants away from densely settled areas. Controlled incineration.
Hydrocarbons and photochemical oxydants including ozone, aldehydes, and PANs	Motor vehicle emission. Solid waste disposal by incineration. Petroleum and chemical industries. Rubber and plastic manufacturing. Evaporation of organic solvents.	Respiratory difficulties. Eye irritation from aldehydes and PAN compounds. Nose and throat irritation from ozone and aldehydes. Photochemical smog. Plant damage.	Better engines and more economical use of fuel.
Carbon monoxide	Incomplete combustion of carbon in fossil fuels, and car exhausts. Forest fires. Petroleum refining. Industrial activities.	Haemoglobin in blood picks up CO thereby reducing its oxygen-carrying capacity which affects the central nervous system and psycho-motor, cardiac, and pulmonary functions. People with emphysema and heart disease highly vulnerable.	Control of automobile exhausts. More use of large public vehicles.
Noise	Transportation vehicles. Urban areas. Industry and mining. Construction activities.	Hearing loss. Psychological effects.	Noise control by better equipment, by buffers such as rows of trees, or by legislation.

around the magnesite ($MgCO_3$) mines of Jhiroli in Almora District of the state of Uttar Pradesh in India. One-third of the workers in the mica mines of Bihar suffer from silicosis. The worst case in India could be the slate pencil factories of Mandsaur in Madhya Pradesh, the sole industrial job provider in the town. The pencils are made by using a cutter on a block of slate in a profusion of silica dust. Most men in the work-force die before the age of 40, and it is difficult to find a woman who has not been widowed at least once.

Silicosis can be avoided by dust control and regular medical examinations, but such measures are not taken in poor and remote areas. This is not an isolated instance: situations of this type occur across the developing world, where poverty and desperation force the workers to take up the sole job opportunity in a remote and poor part of the country, impelling them to work towards an untimely death. The only way to control such exploitation is to raise the consciousness of the people at both the national and local levels about the hazards of air pollution. Asbestos mines provide even grimmer examples, where fine fibres of asbestos are deposited in the lungs, causing pulmonary fibrosis, which ultimately leads to respiratory difficulties and death. The alternative is possible cancer of the lungs or gastro-intestinal tract.

As countries develop economically, their power requirements rise, and in places this need is met by burning low-grade coal. If the coal contains a high amount of impurities, the emission of the power plants becomes a continuous source of air pollution. The burning of sulphur-bearing coal as, for example, in China results in the emission of sulphur dioxide into the atmosphere, which if released in a considerable amount may cause acid rain. In countries with sulphur impurities in coal, acid rain has destroyed vegetation catastrophically and has damaged buildings and statues of historic interest. Even without sulphur impurities, the problem of air pollution from burning of fossil fuels is accentuated when very large power stations are built, like the superthermal power stations of India with an ultimate capacity of more than 2,000 megawatts. The establishment of such super power stations is justified on grounds of economic location, but such economics does not necessarily take into consideration the fact that super power stations are also super sources of air and water pollution. The emission of fly ash with toxic minerals is also potentially a hazardous product of coal-based power stations. In many places the thermal plants either do not have pollution control measures or the existing equipment does not function adequately.

With the development of power plants in the developing countries, a concentrated settlement of workers usually grows up in the immediate vicinity of the power station, close to the source of pollution. The combination of untreated emission of polluted matter from the industry and the concentration of labour in the neighbourhood is extremely common in the Third World countries that are trying to build up an industrial base. Blast furnaces, for example, emit particulates and toxic fumes, but very few of them may have any kind of pollution control measure attached which also functions adequately. Other industries as listed in table 5.1 tend to emit quantities of polluted matter in the air, and frequently are located uncomfortably close to an urban settlement, the growth of which may be connected with the industrial base.

Case study G

Effect of local air pollution on the Taj Mahal

The case of the Taj Mahal is an example of what could be inadvertently destroyed in the course of economic development unless a constant vigil is maintained. This famous mausoleum (plate G.1) is made of Makrana

Plate G.1   The Taj Mahal (Photo: David Drakakis-Smith)

Case study G (*continued*)

marble of pre-Cambrian age, and is of course susceptible to acid corrosion. Several years ago a petroleum refinery was built at Mathura, 40 km away from the Taj at Agra. Several industrial ventures were also started at about the same time in Agra or in the neighbourhood. As a result air pollution increased, and concern was expressed regarding the preservation of this beautiful building. The central government stepped in, a study committee was instituted, and certain of its recommended measures were implemented. Two large thermal power stations and coal-burning locomotives have been removed from Agra. The sulphur dioxide over the city has dropped by 75 per cent. The emission of sulphur dioxide and particulates from the refinery at Mathura is monitored regularly, and given the general pattern of wind movement is said not to be a serious environmental threat to the monument. Some of the recommendations of the committee have not been implemented yet, such as removing 250 or so small iron foundries out of Agra, and planting a green belt around the city as a buffer against possible air pollution from distant sources. The attempt to declare a no-industry zone in Agra unfortunately has not been kindly received either by the local population or by the state government.

This example illustrates two characteristics of industrial pollution. First, it is all pervasive, and second, even if technological solutions exist, their implementation is not easy. The damaged historical monuments of the developed world, where industrial growth and accelerated air pollution made an early appearance, clearly show the results of this.

Population concentration and air pollution

The cities of the Third World have brought together industrial establishments, congested transport systems, and concentrations of people. Such a juxtaposition results in various types of ailments of the lower and upper respiratory system; chronic heart and lung diseases including bronchitis, fibrosis, cancer; and possible eye, nasal, and skin irritation. The pollution of air in these cities is the combined effect of burning coal or firewood for cooking, motor vehicle emission, power station combustion, and the emission from various types of industries.

The problem is becoming more acute in the Third World because of the progressive building of industrial bases, the rapidly developing cities, and the in-migration of the poor to squatter settlements which because of the prevailing poverty are located within walking distance of the place of work. This is a high-risk situation, especially where people are uninformed, where the industry is callous about environmental degradation, and where the government is indifferent or inefficient. Hazardous forms of air pollution may happen anywhere, but in the Third World much of it happens due to neglect of safety measures. Highly toxic and volatile chemicals are stored dangerously; there is little monitoring of the health of workers; and pollution safety measures, such as scrubbers, do not always arrive with the new plant. Such practices are of course found in the other two worlds, but since industrialization is fairly new in the Third World, sensible precautions for the preservation of the environment should be built into the development plans, thereby avoiding both the industrial pollution and the subsequent massive cleaning operations of the developed countries. The more heavily industrialized nations of the Third World are already showing signs of regional concentrations of polluted environment.

Case study H

The disaster at Bhopal

The city of Bhopal, with a population of about 800,000 (figure H.1), is the capital of the state of Madhya Pradesh in central India. In the 1970s Union Carbide established a factory in the northern part of the city, which among other things produced chemicals for pesticides and stored them after production. It was a popular move as it meant jobs for people in town, and provided a means for meeting part of the rising demand for pesticides after the Green Revolution. In the early 1980s there were several leakages and accidents in the plant: warning articles were written in the local press, and representations were made at various levels of the government, but apparently the warnings were not taken seriously by either the plant management or the local government.

About 11.30 pm on the night of 2 December 1984, workers in the Union Carbide plant noticed a gas leak. The leaking gas was methyl isocyanate (MIC), which is used in pesticide manufacturing. The gas leaked out in horrendous quantity. The safety measures were inadequate, and inexplicably the public warning siren of the factory was not properly sounded. By then the highly poisonous MIC gas had spread in a high concentration over 40 km^2 affecting about 200,000 people. People woke up coughing, breathing became impossible, and they started to flee in whatever mode of transport was available: cycles, bullock carts, autorickshaws, cars, buses, trucks.

Case study H (*continued*)

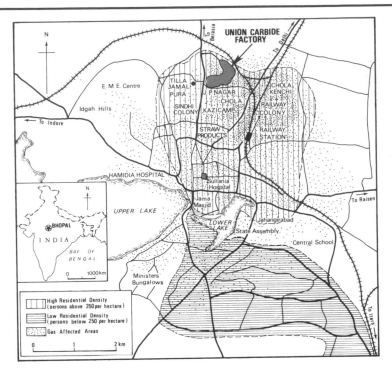

Figure H.1 Bhopal: the spread of the MIC gas [From A. Agarwal and S. Narain (eds) (1986) *The State of India's Environment 1984–85*, New Delhi, Centre for Science and Environment]

Entire families in desperation travelled on a single scooter. People rode the outside of jampacked trucks hanging on to the limbs of people inside. The city streets were jammed with an unending moving stream of humanity. People who found a vehicle to escape on survived, but a very high percentage of those who fled on foot or stayed in their homes did not. The number of people that died is still not exactly known, but the total has

If we extend the lessons of Bhopal to a general level, certain conclusions are reached. The needs of development may require hazardous plants producing toxic fumes, but their establishment should be carefully planned

Case study H (*continued*)

climbed into thousands. If it were not for the fact that the two lakes of Bhopal absorbed a large amount of the MIC gas, the numbers would have been even higher. Particularly badly affected were the poor who lived in shanties near the factory, in houses improvised out of planks, sheets of tin, plastic, and thatch, with gaping holes that the gas could come through. Others were saved by the bravery of the various transport operators who evacuated thousands. The staff at the railway station close to the Union Carbide factory remained at their jobs, waved incoming trains through, and alerted the neighbouring stations to stop trains from coming into Bhopal. Some of the railway staff succumbed to the gas themselves. Eventually units of the Indian army evacuated people systematically.

By the middle of the next day, 25,000 people were crowded into Bhopal's Hamidia Hospital suffering from eye and respiratory ailments. The problem was compounded by the lack of knowledge at that time regarding the specific gas responsible and the information was not forthcoming. The streets of the affected parts of Bhopal were full of vomit and human excreta; the dead lay in gutters, while those who were alive suffered acute physiological distress. The city was full of dead animals, and even the plants were not spared.

The long-term effect of this extreme form of air pollution is not known, but voluntary agencies working in Bhopal have reported that several thousand people are still suffering from respiratory, sleeping, and digestive problems acute enough to make them incapable of carrying out even very light physical jobs. There is a possibility that these people, most of whom were poor manual labourers, will never be able to earn a living. Agarwal and Narain provide a harrowing account of the disaster in their edited book, *The State of India's Environment 1984–85*.

With hindsight, the Bhopal disaster can be attributed to several factors: the storing of a very large volume of an extremely poisonous substance; the safety system that did not work; the inexplicable failure to sound the public warning siren as soon as the gas break was noticed; the late arrival of information to the doctors regarding the type of gas and its antidote; and allowing people to settle close to a hazardous plant.

and monitored. There should be definite policies for siting hazardous factories even though their presence may bring in jobs and economic opportunities in a developing country. Governments should not only have controlling legislations comparable to those anywhere in the world, but also display a willingness to implement them. The possibility of substituting less dangerous materials, a restriction on the amount of toxic material that could be stored, and the adequacy of safety systems in case of accidents should be carefully determined before the plant is installed. The Third World need not carry toxic materials which are severely restricted in the developed countries. Factories which pose a danger to the community should have an uninhabited belt around them. It is not easy to implement such safety measures. The factories bring much-needed income to the local populace; and the poor in the developing countries tend to live as close as possible to the place of work in order to save transportation costs. An industrial plant run by a multinational has tremendous clout in a poor country. As always, coming up with technological solutions to an ecological problem is only a part of the total solution.

Key ideas

1   The major sources of air pollution are transportation, stationary fuel combustion, industry, and disposal of solid wastes.
2   Air pollution in rural areas is mainly from the burning of vegetation, wind action on bare fields, and the burning of firewood inside an enclosed space.
3   Mining is an important source of air pollution, as are thermal power stations.
4   Air pollution in many Third World cities results from domestic burning of coal or fuelwood, motor vehicle emission, power station combustion, and the emission from various types of industries.
5   The effect of air pollution is heightened by the tendency of the workers to live within walking distance of the factories, by the callousness of some industrial firms, and by the indifference of some governments.

6
Urban development and environmental modification

Types of environmental modification

Cities are areas of the greatest alteration of the environment, areas where almost all the effects of ecological modification as a result of development come together. Cities have their own type of climate, vegetation, and surface relief; their own brand of pollution; and their own specialized demands for physical resources. Our world is being progressively urbanized, the number of people living in the towns and cities is rising at a much faster rate than the world population, and increasingly a man-made environment is created replacing the natural one. The rate of urbanization is especially high in the Third World.

The different types of environmental modification that result from urban development can be classified as

1 climatological changes
2 hydrological changes
3 geomorphological changes
4 vegetational changes, and
5 an increase in different types of pollution.

In general, the quality of the environment deteriorates, and the various types of environmental modification occur simultaneously.

Climatological changes

The climate of a city differs in many aspects from that of the surrounding countryside. H.E. Landsberg has summarized our knowledge of this difference (table 6.1). In general, the city, with its built-up areas and human

Table 6.1   Local climatic alterations produced by cities

Elements	*Compared to rural environs*
Contaminants:	
condensation nuclei	10–100 times more
particulates (dust)	10– 50 times more
gaseous admixtures	5– 25 times more
Radiation:	
total on horizontal surface	10–20% less
ultraviolet, low sun	30% less
ultraviolet, high sun	5% less
sunshine duration	5–15% less
Cloudiness:	
clouds	5–10% more
fog, winter	100% more
fog, summer	20–30% more
Precipitation:	
amounts	5–10% more
days with < 5 mm	10% more
Temperature:	
annual mean	0.5–1.0°C more
winter minima (average)	1–2°C more
Surface relative humidity:	
annual mean	6% less
winter	2% less
summer	8% less
Wind speed:	
annual mean	20–30% less
extreme gusts	10–20% less
calms	5–20% more

Source: H.E. Landsberg (1981) 'City climate', in H.E. Landsberg (ed.) *General Climatology, 3*, World Survey of Climatology, vol. 3, Amsterdam, Elsevier.

activities, produces enough heat by combustion, heating, and metabolism to raise the average temperature by a few degrees centigrade. This pattern shows up clearly if one draws regional isotherms, and the term *urban heat island* has been coined to describe such a concentration of heat over urban areas. The heat island effect is more perceptible during daytime and in the first half of the night.

The widespread areal coverage of buildings in close proximity increases the roughness of the city surface which reduces the surface wind speed. The variation of roof heights results in turbulence. The wind circulation pattern of the city, however, is more difficult to establish. The urban heat island effect often results in a convective rise of air over the city bringing in breezes from the countryside. This circulation pattern is strong at night, especially in calm clear weather. The pattern of wind recirculates dust particles, which are plentiful in cities, and a dust dome grows over the settlement resulting in the circulation of atmospheric pollutants over the city centre (figure 6.1). If the city is an area where temperature inversion is common, such as a mountain-girt basin, or where fogs are prevalent as off a cool coast, the pollutant concentration increases.

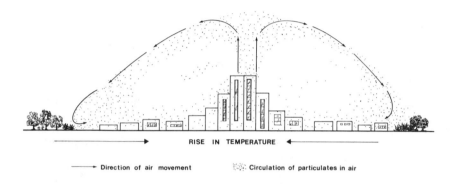

RISE IN TEMPERATURE

→ Direction of air movement   Circulation of particulates in air

Figure 6.1   The urban heat island, air circulation, and the dust dome

The atmospheric pollutants produced by a city are to a large extent solid particles suspended in air but also include gaseous constituents, some of which could have harmful effects. The solids are often hygroscopic, leading to the formation of fogs and reduced visibility, a characteristic which may persist due to the reduction of wind velocity in cities. The concentrations of some common pollutants of urban air are shown in table 6.2.

Landsberg has described air pollution as one of the crucial environmental problems of today's urbanization, which may result in eye irritation, bronchitis, emphysema, and asthma. Very little data exist for the Third World cities, which in itself is worrisome given the rate of urban spread and industrialization, which often results in dense concentrations of population next to main city arteries and near industrial sectors.

Hydrological changes

Wolman has described three stages of hydrological modification of the

Table 6.2 Concentrations of some air pollutants in city atmospheres (in parts per million by volume)

Carbon dioxide	300	–	1,000
Carbon monoxide	1	–	200
Sulphur dioxide	0.01–		3
Oxides of nitrogen	0.01–		1
Aldehydes	0.01–		1
Oxidants, including ozone	0.00–		0.8
Chlorides	0.00–		0.3
Ammonia	0.00–		0.21

Note: This happens with a 10–100 times increase in condensation nuclei, and 10–50 times increase in particulates.

Source: H.E. Landsberg (1981) 'City climate', in H.E. Landsberg (ed.) *General Climatology, 3*, World Survey of Climatology, vol. 3, Amsterdam, Elsevier.

environment occurring from the spread of urban settlements into the countryside:

Stage 1   The countryside before urbanization: land under natural vegetation or agriculture; streams adjusted to the existing conditions of the basin.

Stage 2   The brief period of construction: vegetation is removed; soil and weathered mantle undergo intense erosion; large amount of sediment is released to reach and partially fill drainage channels; streams in disequilibrium resulting from excessive sediment load.

Stage 3   The new urban landscape: construction completed creating an impervious surface of streets, parking lots and roof tops; drainage via concrete drains; increase in flooding; streams still in disequilibrium trying to adjust.

The degree of imperviousness in cities may range from near 20 per cent in low density residential areas to about 90 per cent in the central business district (plate 6.1). The rainwater, instead of slowly infiltrating into the ground, rapidly runs off the rooftops, parking lots, and streets into storm sewers and subsequently into major channels. Not only are infiltration and evaporation reduced in cities, but also as a result of the quick accumulation, major channels, either natural or lined, rise more frequently in flood (plate 6.2). The impact on the hydrology of the area from the urban spread can be summarized (table 6.3).

The general model of increased storm peaks and inter-storm low flows is accentuated in the tropics, as tropical rainfall often arrives in the form of brief, intense storms. In such a climatic environment the flooding of the Bukit Timah Valley of Singapore has increased following the urbanization in the basin, where development tends to climb up the tributary valleys in

Plate 6.1   Singapore: intensive urban landuse

Plate 6.2   An urban drainage channel

the form of housing developments. The urban flooding in certain Third World cities has worsened as a result of subsidence which has followed groundwater withdrawal, which was concomitant with city growth. The best studied examples are Mexico City and Bangkok (case study I).

Table 6.3   Modification of the local hydrology by urbanization

1   Increase in flooding: more frequent high flows in both concrete and natural channels.
2   Quicker rise in channels after rainfall.
3   Increase in channel peak velocity.
4   Decrease in the flow between storm runoffs.
5   Generally a lowering of water quality and hydrologic amenities.

Case study I

Urban development, subsidence, and flooding in Bangkok

Bangkok, which has a current population of over 5 million, is located on the floodplain of the Chao Phraya River, about 25 km north of the Gulf of Thailand. Most of the metropolitan area of about 470 km^2 extends across a low backswamp at an elevation of only 0.5 to 1.5 m above mean sea level. Considerable rainfall arrives during the south-western monsoon, which is also the period when the Chao Phraya runs high. The city till now has depended on a series of canals constructed over the last 200 years for drainage into the Chao Phraya. Bangkok suffers from common developmental problems, such as pollution of water and air and expected flooding during the rainy season, but perhaps the greatest hazard at the moment is the effect of subsidence.

The city has grown rapidly since the 1950s, and the demand for water has been met to a large extent by tapping the groundwater resources. The water comes from several sand and silt aquifers within the soft marine sediments including highly compressable clay beds that underlie Bangkok. The water was for both domestic and industrial use, the industries finding it cheaper than the water supplied by the city. Such proliferation of unchecked pumping led to a rapid lowering of the water table causing the shallow aquifers to turn saline to various degrees. The real disaster for Bangkok was ground subsidence which has been carefully monitored, and found to range up to 14 cm per year in south-eastern Bangkok (figure I.1). The effect of this subsidence has been twofold: structural damage and increased flooding.

Structural damage commonly occurs at the junction of pavements with

Case study I (*continued*)

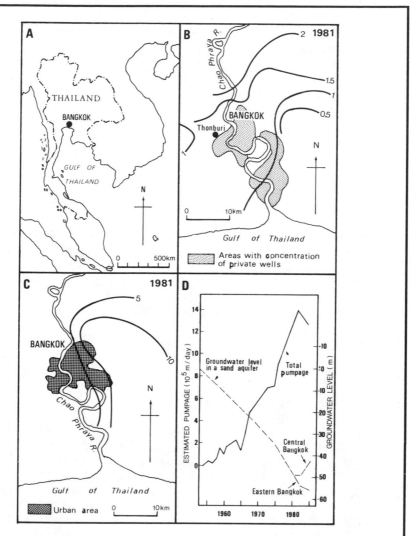

Figure I.1   Groundwater withdrawal and subsidence in Bangkok [Based on J.L. Rau (1986) 'Geotechnical problems in the development of Bangkok', *AGID News*, 49, October, 30–4 and P. Nutalaya and J.L. Rau (1981) 'Bangkok: the sinking metropolis', *Episodes*, 3–7.

Case study I (*continued*)

buildings. The large buildings are on piles and settle at a lower rate than the streets resulting in the development of a prominent set of cracks at the contact. This leads to some of the characteristic features of Bangkok's urban landscape: large buildings require the addition of an extra step below the steps leading to the entrance, sidewalks develop cracks and scarps, well casings protrude above ground surface, and walls open into large cracks one can put an arm through (plate I.1). On the other hand, floods arriving regularly after rainstorms cause shop-owners to build ingenious small-scale embankments to prevent water from pouring into the shop from the streets (plate I.2).

Urban development and subsidence together have increased flooding in Bangkok. It is no longer possible to drain out the water via the canals for various reasons, one of which is the subsidence-created depression of east

Plate I.1   Bangkok: structural damage from subsidence

Case study I (*continued*)

Plate I.2   Bangkok: flood prevention measures

Bangkok. A large number of pumps now move the water from one drainage channel to another, and ultimately over the embankment into the Chao Phraya. The gradients of the canals have been lessened by subsidence, and they are also choked with the city sewage. The floodwater that inundates the city of Bangkok is extremely unpleasant.

Admittedly Bangkok's problems are somewhat extreme, but it is relevant to recall that a number of large and rapidly expanding cities of the Third World are located on comparable substratum: Mexico City, Calcutta, Ho-Chi-Minh City, and Jakarta are a few examples. If urban development requires supply from groundwater below the city, a carefully planned and controlled extraction is necessary, as is now being attempted in Bangkok by the imposition of a groundwater act.

Geomorphological changes

Urban expansion may give rise to two different types of geomorphological problems. The sediment associated with construction activities tends to block the channels, which at about the same time are expected to carry greater volumes of floodwater. Such sediment finds its way to an urban river which is often an ephemeral stream with steep hydrographs, insignificant baseflow, and large sediment concentration at certain times (figure 6.2). During high flow the entire channel is under water, but between periods of high flow the stream is a braided one with shallow channels flowing in the middle of flood-deposited coarse sand.

Uncontrolled development up steep slopes may cause slope failures, especially when intense rain falls on a thick layer of weathered material. Landslides from intense rain have been repeatedly reported from Hong Kong, Singapore, and Rio de Janeiro. Instances of fill slopes even being liquefied in heavy rain and failing have occurred. A standard scenario for such disasters is fairly common. Cities often develop on lower plains either next to or surrounded by steep hillslopes. Pressure on land forces settlement on steep slopes. The poor may build squatter settlements and small farms on the steep hillsides, whereas the rich live in townships away from the polluted city air and with wide open vistas. Such steep slopes are often potentially hazardous due to a combination of unstable geological conditions and unfavourable geomorphic environment such as steep and active alluvial fans. The arrival of a tropical disturbance with intense rain acts as the trigger.

Cities built in naturally hazardous areas are, as expected, prone to disastrous landslides, floods, channel modification, and destruction of people and property. The naturally hazardous areas include regions of high relief, seismically active belts, and areas exposed to the threat of tropical cyclones. Some cities face all three as in Indonesia, the Philippines, Central America, or the West Indies. The spread of urbanization in such areas has to be especially carefully planned.

Pollution in cities

The different types of pollution discussed earlier in this book – excessive sediment, dirty water, toxic air – are all found in cities, often in a concentrated form and in extremely close vicinity to the city-dwellers. The sediment is associated with construction activities, landslides, or slope wash and usually affects specific areas within the urban settlements. Besides increased sedimentation and flooding, urbanization also affects the quality of the local water. The source of the pollution is the domestic and industrial wastes which reach the streams or groundwater. This happens across the

RIVER BEHAVIOUR IN NON-URBAN AREAS:
Usually some water (baseflow)
between peaks associated with rainfall
events. Rise to peak after the rain has
fallen for some time, and a gentle fall
in river level afterwards.

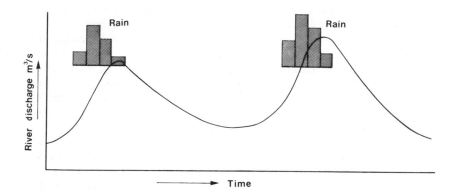

RIVER BEHAVIOUR IN URBAN AREAS:
Very little baseflow. Sharp rise to
peak soon after the rain has started,
and steep fall. Higher peaks.
Floodprone conditions.

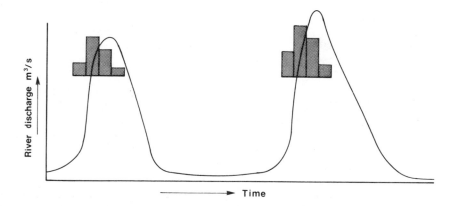

Figure 6.2   Comparison of hydrographs: rural and urban cases

world. Data from the developing world are extremely rare, but given the large number of squatter settlements without proper supply of drinking water or sanitary conditions, the urban streams can be expected to be greatly polluted. Where some data exist, even large rivers like the Ganga show a very high level of pollution, a very large proportion of which comes from untreated human and animal wastes.

The pollution of the air, as described in the previous chapter, becomes hazardous in the city because of the combination of high density population and the concentration of pollutants. The concentration of airborne pollutants increases due to heavy traffic, industrial activity, and combustion. The use of coal and firewood for cooking and heating in the Third World pollutes the air even indoors. The need for proper sewage treatment plants and safe drinking water has been accepted as a desired goal for the Third World cities. As these cities develop in size and as industrial functions come in, it is imperative to monitor the water and the air of such cities, practices which are seldom carried out.

Key ideas

1   The cities of the Third World are rapidly increasing in area and size of population.
2   Cities are areas of the greatest alteration of the environment.
3   Urban rivers or drainage channels are flood prone.
4   Urban development on steep slopes, especially in areas with torrential rain, may cause disastrous landslides.
5   Pollution of land, water, and air is common in urban areas.

Environmental problems and the Third World development

A brief recapitulation

Two sets of observations run through the text of this book. First, development in the Third World has left a series of environmental problems; and second, the environment operates as an integrated system and any type of modification, even if it is local in nature, may start a chain of events resulting in multifarious effects regional in scale. Examples of this can be seen in some of the cases discussed: the deforestation of the tropical rainforest, construction of dams across rivers, and groundwater depletion to meet urban demands.

It should be pointed out that different types of environmental degradations may arrive with different types of economic activities. Air pollution, for example, occurs where a large amount of fuel combustion and industrial activity take place. In that sense, the chapters in this book are arranged progressively in order of more complicated and extensive environmental degradation. Most Third World countries suffer from the effects of extraction or expansion of agriculture to marginal areas. Only the more technologically advanced and populated ones pollute the water and the air to a high degree. The non-uniform availability of information must also be noted. A high frequency of examples from a country not only indicates that cases of environmental degradation are common, but also that such ecological modifications are known, perhaps are being monitored, or even that some preventive measures are being taken. One essential step towards preventing environmental degradation is awareness and involvement at various levels. National governments, provincial and local administrations, academics, the legal profession, the press, the business community, and the local inhabitants all have to live in the area of the ecological deprivation.

Development and environmental protection

Over the last two decades, the countries of the Third World have become increasingly aware of the dangers inherent in unchecked and large-scale development projects. The task of developing a country is perhaps no longer viewed as an exercise in applied economics carried out with help from the engineers. It has now become even politically acceptable to consider the environment.

The 1972 United Nations Conference on the Human Environment held in Stockholm was instrumental in bringing countries together to consider the future of our planet. There was the beginning of a global environmental consciousness, but it also became clear that the protection of the environment in the Third World is not possible so long as the countries remain poor. One oft-quoted remark of Indira Gandhi was that poverty is the greatest polluter. Development is thus related to the improvement of both economic and environmental conditions. The term 'ecodevelopment', attributed to Maurice Strong and currently in frequent use, conveys this approach. The establishment of the United Nations Environmental Programme (UNEP) in Nairobi is associated with development and environmental conservation. Environmental degradation in the Third World is due to several factors: pollution and toxic waste disposal problems due to industrialization; the increased pressure on the environment due to activities such as farming of marginal lands and gathering of fuelwood by the poor; and the extraction of natural resources for either national consumption or use in the developed countries. The deforestation of the south-east Asian rainforest to support the timber industries of Japan, a country with an excellent national forest management record, is a good example. Another type of environmental degradation is the Third World's import of pesticides which are deemed to be too dangerous for use in the countries where they are manufactured.

The machinery for environmental protection

Development programmes, which take into consideration the possible negative environmental impacts and take steps to reduce or prevent them, are thus desirable for the Third World. Apart from the need for technical knowledge, and long-term data on environmental conditions, the developing countries need strict legislation to deal with environmental degradation such as air and water pollution. Such legislation already exists in some Third World countries. Furthermore, the countries should have government agencies with money, clout, and technical expertise to evaluate, monitor, and if necessary, modify or restrain projects for development. This is not always forthcoming, even in the developed countries. Lastly, the importance of the contributions of the voluntary non-government organizations (NGOs) in preventing ecological degradation has been repeatedly demonstrated. Such groups occur at various levels, from grassroots to international, with different interests and capabilities. Their existence at different levels, but with some in-between linkages, is necessary to identify a local ecological problem, technically evaluate it, and draw the attention of the people and government to it. For example at the grassroots level the *Chipko* or the *Appiko* movement of India has prevented deforestation on steep slopes by outsiders armed with tree-felling contracts, by the simple and expeditious technique of hugging the trees when they are about to be felled. The movement has drawn regional and national attention to the problem of deforestation, soil erosion, and increased flooding.

There is an element of chance and local politics in the prevention of possible environmental deterioration associated with the setting up of an industry or a large-scale hydro-electric project, as illustrated by the case of Silent Valley.

Case study J

Silent Valley

Silent Valley is the narrow valley of the Kunthi river in the state of Kerala in south-western India, at an elevation between 2,400 m and 1,000 m. Apart from its scenic appearance, the valley has 8,950 ha of rainforest with valuable rare plants and animals, including the lion-tailed macaque, a threatened primate. The narrow gorge at the lower end of the valley has been considered several times over a number of years as a possible site for generating hydro-electricity. In 1973 the then state government of Kerala wanted to dam the gorge, fill a reservoir upstream which would have drowned out a large part of the invaluable rainforest, and generate power. The project, however, was delayed till 1976.

By that time the attention of several people in prominent positions and with an interest in conservation had been drawn to the Silent Valley project. They included officers in the central government in New Delhi and a government ecological task force. The task force report queried the cost estimates of the project, was unhappy about the submergence of the forest, and wondered whether the proposed generation of only 120 megawatts of power justified the destruction of such a unique environment. About that

Case study J (*continued*)

time a group of school and college teachers and scientists of Kerala started a protest against the project on the grounds of environmental despoilation.

The project by this time was being attacked by various Indian and international conservation groups, resulting in attempts by the state government to rush the project through. The state assembly passed a unanimous resolution for the speedy implementation of the hydro-electric project. The implementation of the project was delayed by scientific controversy, several court orders, and the fact that approval was needed from the central government. While all these were being sorted out, Indira Gandhi returned to the premiership in early 1980 and, being sympathetic to conservationist issues, referred the project to a new scientific committee which in 1983 came out in favour of conservation.

Silent Valley has become a landmark in the ecological movements, where a Third World group of conservationists prevented the state government from destroying a valuable rainforest. It is, however, salutary to note that the success of the movement was due to the fortuitous coming together of several conservationist groups at various levels, local, national, international; the willingness of some scientists to examine the issue and take a stand on their findings; the publicity generated; and when the time for the final decision arrived the Prime Minister happened to be a person interested in environmental protection. There is an element of chance in the protection of the environment.

The model of large-scale development may not be appropriate for everybody and technology has to meet the scale of the demand and the environment. Small, even if not always, is sometimes beautiful. Water management in the irrigated rice areas of Bali is carried out by the *subak*, an irrigation association which has been in existence for centuries. The members of the associations are farmers who grow irrigated rice, and collectively under an elected head are responsible for monitoring the irrigation conduits and the infrastructure, and managing the crop pattern. The organization is an independent entity, but works in co-ordination with the infrastructure of the local government. The fields of Bali have thus been efficiently supplied with water for hundreds of years without the need for a large-scale engineering project.

The future trends

In recent years there has been a heightening of the awareness towards environmental protection in the Third World. Development and protection of the environment are more readily accepted as interrelated, even though one or both of them might have to be dealt with on a crisis footing. As the countries of the Third World are industrialized, they inherit problems similar to those of the developed countries. On the other hand, there is a diffusion of technology and management from such countries regarding environmental problem-solving in the Third World.

A common problem for a number of the Third World countries is the pressure on them to service their international debt. As a result some countries tend to over-exploit their natural resources, a situation which has been recently discussed by Myers. The two examples given by Myers are cattle ranching and the easing of logging restrictions in the tropical rainforest. The burden of the international debt is also behind the use of farmlands for non-food crops for export commodities, thereby pushing the poor farmers on to the marginal areas. It is interesting to note that multilateral development banks (MDBs) such as the World Bank or the African Development Bank have been criticized for lending money on projects which would lead to environmental degradation. The colonization project of Polonoroeste, which involved degradation of the Amazon rainforest by highway construction and controlled migration, is a case in point. The conflict between development and environmental protection, or between the interests of the developed and developing countries, is due to overlooking the fact that there is only one earth. If rainforests are to be preserved for the sake of the world, it is necessary to provide technical and financial help to the countries that still have the rainforests, so that development is possible without uncontrolled deforestation. As a recent World Resources Institute Report has stated, the development assistance agencies could do more. The average annual lending by all development banks over the 1980–4 period has been only US$100 million for forestry, compared to a total of over US$20,000 million. The four banks (World Bank, Inter-American Development Bank, Asian Development Bank, and African Development Bank) have less than 1 per cent of their annual financing allocated to forestry, the UN Development Programme slightly better with 2 per cent. It is the short-term development efforts that take precedence. Recently, however, the President of the World Bank has announced various measures, including an expansion of annual lending, to protect the environment of the developing countries.

In March 1985 the Supreme Court of India, on petition from the citizens of the Doon Valley in the fragile environment of the Kumaun Himalayas, declared that a large number of limestone quarries of the valley be closed on grounds of environmental degradation. According to the judgment this has to be done in the interest of protecting and safeguarding the right of the people to live in a healthy environment with minimal disturbance of ecological balance. This historic judgment indicates that uncontrolled development cannot take precedence over environmental protection. Growth of per capita income, equity of resources, and sustainability of the environment are simultaneously required in the Third World.

Key ideas

1   Development is related to the improvement of both economic and environmental conditions.
2   Development programmes should take into consideration the possible degrading environmental impacts and take steps to avoid or reduce such problems.
3   Environmental protection is possible only when backed by legislation, government machinery, and public awareness and participation.
4   There is an element of chance in the protection of the environment.
5   There is a heightening of the awareness towards environmental protection in the Third World.
6   There is only one earth; we all share its resources.

Review questions and further reading

Chapter 1

Further reading

Carson, R. (1962) *Silent Spring*, Harmondsworth, Penguin.
Eckholm, E.P. (1978) *Losing Ground*, Oxford, Pergamon.
Marsh, G.P. (1898) *The Earth as Modified by Human Agencies: A Last Revision of 'Man and Nature'*, New York, Charles Scribner & Sons.

Chapter 2

1 Where is relatively undisturbed natural vegetation found in the Third World? How many of such areas are under the threat of deforestation? What type of land use will replace the natural vegetation in such areas?
2 Why is the issue of fuelwood so important in the Third World? What kind of hardship is caused by a scarcity of fuelwood? Is there any viable alternative?
3 The degradation of the environment as a result of deforestation is felt at various levels: local, regional, global. What are such effects of deforestation?
4 What is the role of First World organizations in the deforestation of the Third World?

Further reading

Agarwal, A. and Narain, S. (eds) (1986) *The State of India's Environment 1984–85: The Second Citizens' Report*, New Delhi, Centre for Science and Environment.

Jackson, P. (1983) 'The tragedy of our tropical rainforests', *Ambio* 12 (5), 252–4.

Myers, N. (1986) 'Economics and ecology in the international arena: the phenomenon of linked linkages', *Ambio* 15 (5), 296–300.

Salati, E. and Vose, P.B. (1983) 'Depletion of tropical rain forests', *Ambio* 12 (2), 67–71.

World Resources Institute (1985) *Tropical Forests: Call for Action*, Washington, DC, World Resources Institute.

Chapter 3

1   What are the factors that cause pressure on land in the Third World?
2   Where are the marginal lands located in the Third World?
3   How does the Green Revolution work? Does it cause any environmental problems? Has the Green Revolution been successful?
4   What is the proper way to bring irrigated water to dry lands?
5   What is desertification and where does it happen? Is there a solution?
6   What are the effects of deforestation and cultivation on steep slopes? Are the effects all local? What parts of the world are affected by cultivation on steep slopes?

Further reading

Eckholm, E.P. (1978) *Losing Ground*, Oxford, Pergamon.

Chapter 4

1   What are the different types of water use? How does demand for water change with improving economic conditions?
2   Why is safe drinking water so important for the Third World? How prevalent is the supply of potable water? What is the indirect benefit of bringing water close to the inhabitants of the Third World?
3   Select a few Third World cities, and determine their possible sources of water supply.
4   How do rivers purify themselves of organic wastes? Select a large river flowing through the Third World countries, and determine how many cities may use it both for supply of drinking water and disposal of waste water.

5 What are the major sources of water pollution? Choose a Third World country to investigate this.
6 Select a major project on a Third World river, and tabulate the benefits and problems arising out of the project. Are there any possible solutions to the problems?

Further reading

Biswas, A.K. (1978) 'Water development and environment', in B.N. Lohani and N.C. Thanh (eds) *Water Pollution Control in Developing Countries*, vol. 2, Bangkok, Asian Institute of Technology.
Dunne, T. and Leopold, L.B. (1978) *Water in Environmental Planning*, San Francisco, Calif., W.H. Freeman.
Hammerton, D. (1972) 'The Nile River – a case history', in R.T. Oglesby, C.A. Carlson, and J.A. McCann (eds) *River Ecology and Man*, New York, Academic Press.
Kishk, M.A. (1986) 'Land degradation in the Nile Valley', *Ambio* 15 (4), 226–30.

Chapter 5

1 What are the different types of air pollutants? List their sources and effects.
2 Why is indoor air pollution common in the Third World?
3 Select a Third World country with considerable mining activities. How much air pollution near the mines would you expect? What are your suggestions for dealing with such problems?
4 Air in certain Third World cities is highly polluted: Mexico City, Bangkok, Calcutta, for example. Choose one such city and describe the causes of such pollution. Can you suggest any remedial measure?
5 How would you ensure that a Bhopal-type disaster will not happen again in the Third World?

Further reading

Agarwal, A. and Narain, S. (eds) (1986) *The State of India's Environment 1984–85: The Second Citizens' Report*, New Delhi, Centre for Science and Environment.
Miller, G.T., jun. (1986) *Environmental Science: An Introduction*, Belmont, Calif., Wadsworth.

Chapter 6

1 In what ways does the physical environment of a city differ from that of the countryside?

2   How does the building of a city modify the local climate? What effect does it have on the well-being of the citizens?
3   Urbanization is followed by an increase in flooding of urban drainage channels. How does this happen? What steps would you suggest to ameliorate such flooding?
4   Explain how the Third World cities bring people and pollution together.
5   Rapid urbanization is expected in the Third World. What effect would it have on the environment about fifty years from today?

Further reading

Douglas, I. (1985) 'Urban sedimentology', *Progress in Physical Geography*, 9 (2), 255–80.
Gupta, A. (1984) 'Urban hydrology and sedimentation in the humid tropics', in J.E. Costa and P.J. Fleisher (eds) *Developments and Applications of Geomorphology*, Heidelberg, Springer-Verlag.
Landsberg, H.E. (1981) 'City climate', in H.E. Landsberg (ed.) *General Climatology, 3*, World Survey of Climatology, vol. 3, Amsterdam, Elsevier.
Leopold, L.B. (1968) 'Hydrology for urban land planning', *U.S. Geological Survey Circular 554*.
Rau, J.L. and Nutalaya, P. (1982) 'Geomorphology and land subsidence in Bangkok, Thailand', in R.G. Craig and J.L. Craft (eds) *Applied Geomorphology*, London, Allen & Unwin.
Wolman, M.G. (1967) 'A cycle of sedimentation and erosion in urban river channels', *Geografiska Annaler*, 49A, 385–95.

Chapter 7

1   Why should development of an area take into consideration the environmental conditions?
2   What are the factors that degrade environment in the Third World? Does the Third World have control over all of them?
3   What machinery should we have to protect the environment in the Third World? At what level?
4   How would you describe the future trends towards environmental protection in the Third World?

Further reading

D'Monte, D. (1985) *Temples or Tombs*, New Delhi, Centre for Science and Environment.
Myers, N. (1986) 'Economics and ecology in the international arena: the phenomenon of "linked linkages" ', *Ambio* 15 (5), 296–300.

Index

5821